BEN GOLDSTEIN
CERI JONES

The BIG Picture

ELEMENTARY B

Student's Book

Richmond

Richmond

Richmond Publishing ®
58 St Aldates
Oxford
OX1 1ST
United Kingdom

© Santillana Educación, S.L./Richmond Publishing

First Edition: 2011 / Reprinted: 2013
Split Edition: 2014

Publisher: Deborah Tricker
Managing Editor: Mary Todd
Development Editor: Eleanor Clements
Content Development: Laura Miranda
'Skills Development' Sections: Verity Cole
Progress Tests: Daniel Barber
Proofreaders: Rachel Unsworth, Hazel Geatches
Cover Design: Pentacor Book Design, Lorna Heaslip
Design & Layout: Lorna Heaslip, Rob Briggs, Dave Kuzmicki
Photo Researcher: Magdalena Mayo
Art Coordinators: Lorna Heaslip, Dave Kuzmicki
Illustrators: Richard Allen c/o Eye Candy Illustration Ltd., Francis Blake c/o Three-in-a-Box Ltd., Chris Davidson, Andy Davies c/o Eye Candy Illustration Ltd., Jonny Hannah c/o Heart Illustration Ltd., Roger Harris c/o N.B. Illustration Ltd., Paul Oakley, Optical 3D Ltd., Graham White c/o N.B. Illustration Ltd., Ron Wilson, Zap Art c/o N.B. Illustration Ltd., William Donohoe, Dylan Gibson c/o Eye Candy Illustration Ltd., Phil Hackett c/o Eye Candy Illustration Ltd., Sylvie Pinsonneaux c/o Eye Candy Illustration Ltd., Ben Swift
Audio Production: Motivation Sound Studios

Photos – Student's Book:

C. Jiménez/photoAlquimia; I. Codina; J. Jaime; J. M.ª Escudero; J. Rosselló; J. V. Resino; M. Blanco; M. Fernández; Prats i Camps; S. Enríquez; S. Padura; M. Mayo; James Silverman; FLICKR/Jack French, Bondiben, Rolland Budi, Todd Smith, Trevor To, Aldoaldoz; A. G. E. FOTOSTOCK; ACI AGENCIA DE FOTOGRAFÍA; Bossaball Sports SL; Bridgeman Art Library; EFE/AIRBUS/HANDOUT; EFE/SIPA-PRESS/Isabelle Simon, Martin Sasse; Tony Cenicola/New York Times/Redux/EYEVINE; GETTY IMAGES SALES SPAIN/Photos.com Plus; HIGHRES PRESS STOCK/AbleStock.com; I. Preysler; Bakke-Svensson/Ironman; ISTOCKPHOTO; MOTORING PICTURE LIBRARY/T. Wood; PANOS PICTURES/Dieter Telemans, Trygve Bolstad, Aubrey Wade, Natalie Behring, Lorena Ros, Jeroen Oerlemans, Mark Henley; PHOTODISC; SEIS X SEIS; REX FEATURES/Patrick Frilet, Nils Jorgensen, Richard Jones, George Konig, Sipa-Press, Rawan, Geoff Wilkinson, ALAMY, Evening Standard/Barry Phillips, Masatoshi Okauchi, Nicholas Bailey; MATTON-BILD; Nokia Corporation; P. Moral; PA Photos; PHILIPS; REUTERS/CORBIS/Miguel Vidal; Samsung; SERIDEC PHOTOIMAGENES CD; StockFood/Baranowski, Andre; Twitter, Inc.; Urban Space Management Ltd; www.internationalwomensday.com; www.seanazul.com; ARCHIVO SANTILLANA

Photos – Workbook:

C. Díez Polanco; D. Lezama; GARCÍA-PELAYO/Juancho; J. Jaime; J. Lucas; J. M.ª Escudero; S. Enríquez; COMSTOCK; GETTY IMAGES SALES SPAIN/Photos.com

Plus; HIGHRES PRESS STOCK/ AbleStock.com; I. Preysler; ISTOCKPHOTO/Amanda Rohde; MELBA AGENCY; PHOTODISC; SEIS X SEIS; Alamy; Cortesía de Apple; CREATIVE LABS; Nokia Corporation; SERIDEC PHOTOIMAGENES CD; ARCHIVO SANTILLANA

Cover Photo:
Housing development, aerial view: São Paulo, Brazil
Getty Images Sales Spain/Superstudio

We would like to thank the following reviewers for their valuable feedback which has made *The Big Picture* possible. We extend our thanks to the many teachers and students not mentioned here.

(Argentina): Cecilia Chiacchio, Ingrid Suhring; (Brazil): Ana Falcao, Virginia Garcia, Patricia McKay, Cynthia Phillipps; (Colombia): Kathleen Canal; (Italy): Morgan Cox, Karen Geiger, Sarah Stats; (Mexico): Emma Dominguez, Melissa Ferrin, Lupita Neve, Coral Ibarra Yunez; (Poland): Malgosia Adams, Marta Rosinska; (Spain): Vicki Anderson, Juan Carlos Araujo, Karen Dyer, Gabby Maguire, Fiona McClelland, Karin Rickatson, Eva Sabater, Almudena Verdugo Valcarce, Merce Vilarrubias, Andy Walsh; (UK): Cathy Ellis, Howard Smith, Jonathan Stoddart

Every effort has been made to trace the holders of copyright, but if any omissions can be rectified, the publishers will be pleased to make the necessary arrangements.

Dados Internacionais de Catalogação na Publicação (CIP)
(Câmara Brasileira do Livro, SP, Brasil)

Goldstein, Ben
    The big picture, elementary : student´s book/workbook /
Ben Goldstein, Ceri Jones. -- São Paulo :
Moderna, 2014. -- (The big picture)

    1. Inglês - Estudo e ensino I. Jones, Ceri.
II. Título. III. Série.

13-13475   CDD-420.7

Índices para catálogo sistemático:
1. Inglês : Estudo e ensino 420.7

978-85-16-09144-6

All rights reserved.

No part of this work may be reproduced, stored in a retrieval system or transmitted in any form, electronic, mechanical, photocopying or otherwise without the prior permission in writing of the copyright holders.

RICHMOND PUBLISHING
EDITORA MODERNA LTDA.
Rua Padre Adelino, 758 — Belenzinho
São Paulo — SP — Brasil — CEP 03303-904
Central de atendimento ao usuário: 0800 771 8181
www.richmond.com.br
2013

Printed in Brazil

UNITS 7–12

CONTENTS

	GRAMMAR	VOCABULARY	READING & LISTENING	PRONUNCIATION

7 GOING PLACES
page 72

- Past simple: *to be*
- Past simple: regular & irregular verbs
- Uses of the past simple

- The weather
- Transport

- R Paradise lost
- Text messages
- L Weather report
- Visit to Benidorm
- A rainy day
- Transport to work

- Past tense /ed/ endings
- Sentence stress

page 80 **FUNCTIONAL LANGUAGE:** USING PUBLIC TRANSPORT   *page 81* **SPEAKING TASK:** A PROGRAMME FOR A DAY OUT
page 155 **WRITING BANK:** AN EMAIL TO A FRIEND

8 IN THE NEWS
page 82

- Past simple: irregular verbs & time expressions
- Verb + *to* + infinitive
- Sequencers

- Talking about the news
- Lexical sets
- Collocations

- R The world's oldest blogger
- Australian police arrest French Spider-Man
- L Three news stories
- Radio report about Alain Robert

- Irregular past tense verbs
- Showing interest/ emotion

page 90 **FUNCTIONAL LANGUAGE:** RESPONDING TO NEWS   *page 91* **WRITING TASK:** A LOCAL NEWS STORY

9 HUNGRY PLANET
page 92

- Countable & uncountable nouns
- Quantifiers: *too much/ many, a lot of, a few,* etc

- Food & drink
- Talking about food

- R Article about pasta
- Opinions about a campaign
- L Breakfast around the world
- Explaining an advert

- /ʌ/, /ʊ/, /uː/
- Intonation in questions and requests

page 100 **FUNCTIONAL LANGUAGE:** EATING OUT   *page 101* **SPEAKING TASK:** A DESCRIPTION OF A MEAL
page 156 **WRITING BANK:** REPLY TO A BLOG POST

page 102 **REVIEW C,** UNITS 7–9   *page 105* **BRING IT TOGETHER** 7, 8 & 9

10 STATE OF THE ART
page 106

- Comparative adjectives
- *Going to*
- Personal pronouns

- Technology
- Communication verbs & adjectives

- R Online comments
- Cell phones fighting poverty
- L Advert for an e-reader
- Interview about flash mobs

- Weak form of *going to* /ɡənə/
- Checking understanding

page 114 **FUNCTIONAL LANGUAGE:** GIVING INSTRUCTIONS   *page 115* **WRITING TASK:** A CLASS FORUM

11 A WORKING LIFE
page 116

- Superlative adjectives
- *Will/Won't*
- *Will & might*

- Work & jobs
- Work conditions

- R Hairdressers: the happiest profession
- Top ten predictions: the world of work
- L Radio show about island caretaker job

- *will*: in questions, short answers & for emphasis
- Stress in offers & requests

page 124 **FUNCTIONAL LANGUAGE:** OFFERS & REQUESTS   *page 125* **SPEAKING TASK:** AN ACTION PLAN
page 157 **WRITING BANK:** REPLY TO AN ONLINE ADVERT

12 LISTMANIA!
page 126

- Present perfect: *Have you ever...?*
- Present perfect & past simple
- Review of verbs

- Dreams & ambitions
- Review: common verbs & collocations
- Describing places

- R Top ten things to do before you die
- Review of two cities
- L Discussion about books
- Description of two cities
- Ironman World Championship

- *I've lived* vs *I lived*
- Sentence stress

page 134 **FUNCTIONAL LANGUAGE:** FINDING OUT & RECOMMENDING   *page 135* **WRITING TASK:** LANGUAGE LEARNING TIPS

page 136 **REVIEW D,** UNITS 10–12   *page 139* **BRING IT TOGETHER,** 10, 11 & 12

page 146 **GRAMMAR REFERENCE**   *page 155* **WRITING BANK**   *page 158* **COMMUNICATION BANK**   *page 164* **TRANSCRIPTS**   *page 168* **IRREGULAR VERBS**

3

7 Going places

1 a Work in pairs. Match the photos to the places and seasons.
   1 in a city, in the country, in the mountains, on the beach
   2 spring, summer, autumn, winter

   b 💬 What do you notice about the photos? Which place do you like most? Why?

2 🔊 **7.1** Listen to four people describing the places. Which place is each person talking about?

7.0

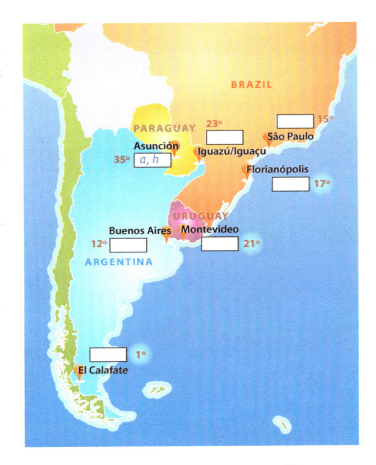

KEY VOCABULARY

The weather

A Match the words in **bold** to the weather symbols. Use a dictionary to help you.

1 It's **raining**. [b]
2 It's **cold**. ☐
3 It's **snowing**. ☐
4 It's **windy** and **cloudy**. ☐☐
5 It's **sunny** and **warm**. ☐☐
6 It's **hot**, really hot. ☐

NOTICE TALKING ABOUT THE WEATHER

When we talk about the weather we use *it + be*:
It's cold. It's raining. It's cloudy.

B Look at the words in **bold** in transcript 7.2 on page 164. Use them to complete the thermometer.

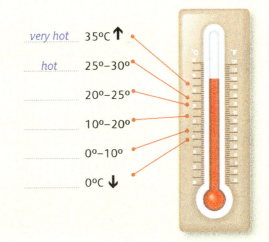

very hot   35°C ↑
hot   25°–30°
....   20°–25°
....   10°–20°
....   0°–10°
....   0°C ↓

NOTICE WEATHER ADJECTIVES

Some weather adjectives come from nouns:
rain → rainy   cloud → cloudy
wind → windy   snow → snowy

When a noun has one syllable and ends in consonant–vowel–consonant, we double the final consonant:
sun → sunny   fog → foggy

When a noun ends in *-e*, we replace the *-e* with *-y*:
ice → icy

3 Complete **A** in the KEY VOCABULARY PANEL ▇.

4 💬 Discuss the questions with a partner.
- Where do you prefer to go on holiday: the city, the country, the mountains or the beach?
- Does it depend on the weather? Or the season?

In spring I like going to the mountains – it's usually warm and sunny, and the mountains are full of flowers.

5 🔊 7.2 Listen to a weather forecast for South America. Write the correct weather symbol(s), a–h, from **A** next to each town on the map above.

6 Work in pairs to complete **B** in the KEY VOCABULARY PANEL ▇.

7 a Find four more adjectives in transcript 7.2 on page 164 to describe the weather. Can you use them to describe the climate in your home town?

b 💬 Work in pairs or small groups. Discuss the questions.
- What's the weather like where you live at the moment?
- Do you like this kind of weather? Why/Why not?

73

7.1 BEFORE AND AFTER

- PRACTISE THE PAST SIMPLE: *TO BE*
- DESCRIBE PLACES IN THE PAST & NOW

Paradise Lost

1 You're looking at Dreamland beach in Bali. My favourite holiday destination. Or at least it **was** when I **was** first there in 1985. There **were** mostly local people and fishermen. There **weren't** many visitors. It **was** a great place to chill out and relax. It **was** good to have a meal in the local restaurants (*warungs*). It **was** perfect for swimming and surfing. And it **was** cheap! And as for the beach… what can I say? **Was** this paradise? Yes, it **was**! Or at least it **was** my idea of paradise. It **was** perfect, a long stretch of turquoise water and empty white sand.

2 I **was** there on holiday again in the 1990s. There **were** more foreign tourists, but that **wasn't** a problem. It **was** never crowded. It **was** still a great place for a quiet, relaxing holiday.

3 Twenty-five years later and Bali is very different. I'm standing here at the top of my favourite beach. And it just doesn't look the same. They're finishing the last hotel at Dreamland. I can't believe my eyes. The *warungs* aren't there anymore. Now there's a big, busy road, and an expensive 18-hole golf course. There are lots of new hotels, luxury villas and condominiums. Today there are many tourists and it's dirty and noisy. Everything is commercial and modern. It's not a dream land anymore! Back in 1985, Dreamland **was** a good name, but now it isn't dreamland – it's just a nightmare.

READING

1 💬 Look at the photos. They show a beach resort in Bali. Which photo do you like the most? Why?

2 Read the blog about Dreamland. Match the captions to the four photos.
   1 Building Dreamland
   2 Dreamland as it was
   3 Dreamland in the 1990s
   4 Dreamland today

3 What is the blog saying? Tick the correct sentence.
   1 Dreamland is wonderful now.
   2 The island of Bali is not very different now.
   3 Not all the changes to Dreamland are bad.
   4 Commercial interests change beautiful places.

4 <u>Underline</u> the positive words in paragraphs 1 and 2, and the negative words in paragraph 3.

5 💬 Do you agree that all the changes to Dreamland are negative? Can you think of a positive side to the changes?

7.1

Grammar

1 Work in pairs. Look at the verbs in **bold** in paragraphs 1 and 2 of the blog. Complete 1–7 in the GRAMMAR PANEL with the verbs.

2 a Look at the two photos of Benidorm in Spain today and 60 years ago. Complete the sentences with the correct form (present or past) of the verb *to be*.

1 Before, there .... any big hotels.
2 Today, there .... lots of hotels.
3 Then, there .... many tourists.
4 Now, there .... lots of people.
5 The beach .... quiet in the past.
6 The beach .... quiet now.
7 Now, the view .... very pretty.
8 Then, the landscape .... really beautiful.

b Work in pairs. Think of three more sentences.

3 Work in small groups. Think of a place you know well which was very different in the past. Tell your group about it. What was it like in the past? What things are different now?

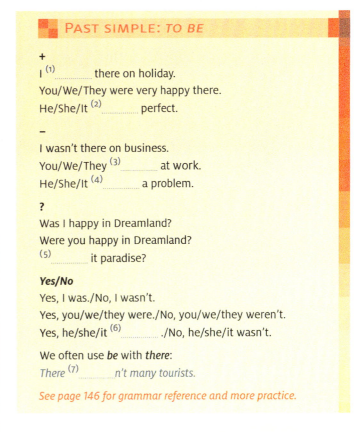

PAST SIMPLE: *TO BE*

+
I (1) .... there on holiday.
You/We/They were very happy there.
He/She/It (2) .... perfect.

–
I wasn't there on business.
You/We/They (3) .... at work.
He/She/It (4) .... a problem.

?
Was I happy in Dreamland?
Were you happy in Dreamland?
(5) .... it paradise?

Yes/No
Yes, I was./No, I wasn't.
Yes, you/we/they were./No, you/we/they weren't.
Yes, he/she/it (6) ..../No, he/she/it wasn't.

We often use *be* with **there**:
There (7) .... n't many tourists.

See page 146 for grammar reference and more practice.

Listening & Speaking

1 🔊 7.3 Listen to Adam describing a visit to Benidorm. Was it a good trip? Why/Why not? What does he think of the town?

2 a Read the sentences below. Who is speaking, Adam (A) or his friend Will (W)?

1 How was your trip?
2 It was great, thanks, really great.
3 It wasn't all bad.
4 It was lovely in the past.
5 It was very busy.
6 The hotel was nice. There was a great pool and a sea view.
7 It was hot and sunny.
8 We were on the beach every day!

b Listen again and check.

3 a 💬 Work in pairs. Think of a trip to a town or city. Tell your partner about the trip and the place. Start your description like this.

I want to tell you about a trip to…
I was there…
It was…

b As you listen, ask your partner questions about the trip.

Was it a good trip?
What was the weather like?

7.2 RAINY DAYS

- PRACTISE THE PAST SIMPLE: REGULAR & IRREGULAR VERBS
- TALK ABOUT WHAT HAPPENED IN THE PAST

LISTENING

1 Work in small groups. Look at the photos and discuss the questions.
- What are the people doing?
- What do you usually do when it rains?

2 7.4 Listen to Lola talking about a rainy day. Which photos go with her story?

3 a Work in pairs. Which of the verbs in the box does Lola not talk about?

> eating pizza   going to the cinema   having coffee
> having a shower   playing cards   playing volleyball
> sitting on the bus   swimming   waiting   walking

b Listen again and check.

GRAMMAR

1 a Work in pairs. Read the extracts from transcript 7.4. Put them in the correct order.
- a We missed the bus.
- b We didn't want to wait for a bus in the rain.
- c It started to rain.
- d We decided to go home.
- e We walked... all the way home.
- f We went out for a pizza.
- g We had a coffee.
- h We played a couple of games of cards.
- i Did you call a taxi? No, we didn't.

b Check your answers in transcript 7.4 on page 164.

2 Underline all the verbs in the sentences in 1a and complete 1–9 in the GRAMMAR PANEL.

3 a Complete the dialogue using the verbs in brackets in the past simple.

A What (1) _did you do_ (you/do) at the weekend?
B We (2) _____ (want) to get away, so we went to the country.
A Where (3) _____ (you/go)?
B To the mountains. We (4) _____ (stay) in a campsite.
A Nice. (5) What _____ (you/do)?
B We (6) _____ (go) walking in the mountains, we (7) _____ (have) a barbecue. It (8) _____ (rain) a bit on Sunday. What about you?
A Nothing special. I (9) _____ (work) on Saturday. I (10) _____ (need) to finish that report. On Sunday I (11) _____ (stay) in and (12) _____ (relax). I (13) _____ (watch) some television, I (14) _____ (do) some cooking – you know, the usual.
B That's boring!
A No, you're wrong. That's what rainy Sundays are for!

b 7.5 Listen and check. Whose weekend do you prefer? Why?

4 Write questions in the past simple. Then ask and answer them with a partner.
1 What/do last weekend?
2 stay at home?
3 do anything interesting?
4 Who/see?
5 Where/go?
6 have a good time?

PAST SIMPLE: REGULAR & IRREGULAR VERBS

We use the past simple to talk about actions that happened in the past.

+

To form verbs in the past simple we add *-ed* to the infinitive:
miss – (1) .... , *start* – (2) .... , *walk* – (3) ....

–

We use *didn't* + infinitive for negative verbs:
We (4) .... *want to wait.*

?

We use *did* + **subject** + **infinitive** for questions:
What (5) .... *you do?*
(6) .... *you call a taxi?*

Yes/No

We use *did/didn't* in short answers:
Yes, we did./No, we (7) ....

Some common irregular verbs

The verbs *have*, *do* and *go* have irregular past forms:
go – (8)*w*............... , *do* – *did*, *have* – (9)*h*............... .

See page 146 for grammar reference and more practice.

PRONUNCIATION: Past simple endings

1 a Write the past simple form of the verbs.

1 decide ....   5 need ....
2 play ....   6 stay ....
3 walk ....   7 want ....
4 watch ....   8 work ....

b 🔊 7.6 Listen to both forms of the verbs. Which verbs have an extra syllable in the past simple? Check your answers against the rule below.

When the infinitive of a verb finishes in a /d/ or /t/ sound, we pronounce the past simple *-ed* ending as /ɪd/.

2 💬 Read the sentences. Work in pairs. Are any of them true for your last weekend?

1 I wanted to stay in.
2 I needed to do some work.
3 I watched a film on TV.
4 I played cards with my friends.
5 I decided to do some studying.
6 I walked around town for hours.

SPEAKING

1 a Work in pairs. Look at the photos. Write questions using *When did you last...?*

When did you last play cards?

b 💬 Ask and answer the questions. Were any of your answers the same?

When did you last play cards?
Last weekend. I played cards with my friends in a bar.

NOTICE *LAST*

We use *last* with *night*, *week*, *month*, *year*, etc. to form time expressions:

last night, last week, last month, last year.

You can also use *last* in questions:

When did you last...? = When was the last time you...?

2 a When did you last get caught in the rain? Read the questions and prepare to tell your story. Make notes about what you want to say. Use a dictionary to help you.

- Where were you?
- At home or away?
- When did it start raining?
- Did you get wet?
- Who were you with?
- What did you do?

b 💬 Work in small groups. Tell your stories.

One day I was...

7.3 ALL CHANGE

- PRACTISE USES OF THE PAST SIMPLE
- TALK ABOUT TRANSPORT & TRAVEL

VOCABULARY: Transport

1 Match the words in the box to the photos. Use a dictionary to help you.

bus   plane   bike   boat   train   subway   car
taxi   motorbike/scooter   tram   ferry

2 Work in pairs. Discuss the questions.
- Which forms of transport exist in your home town? Which do you use? How often do you use them?
- Which of these forms of transport do you prefer for everyday life? For short distances? For long distances? Why?
- How many different forms of transport did you use last week? Where did you go?

LISTENING

1 7.7 Listen to four people, Bruno, Erykah, Carole and Alek, talking about changes to the transport they use every day. What two forms of transport does each person talk about?

2 Listen again. Match each speaker to the reason why he/she changed the form of transport.
1 There was no other alternative before.
2 They introduced a new service in his/her town.
3 His/Her job changed.
4 He/She didn't want to cause pollution.

NOTICE BY

We often use *by* + transport:
I go to school by bus.
I went to college by train.

3 a Work in pairs. Rewrite the sentences to make them true.
1 Bruno didn't hate flying before.
2 Erykah had a choice about how to get to school.
3 Carole didn't decide to change her form of transport.
4 Alek preferred the train because it was cheap.

b Check your answers in transcript 7.7 on pages 164–165. How does your daily journey compare?

My journey is short, like Carole's.

7.3

GRAMMAR

1 a Complete the extracts with a past simple verb.

BRUNO	I ⁽¹⁾w............ to work by subway for years because I ⁽²⁾l............ and ⁽³⁾w............ in Rio.
ERYKAH	We ⁽⁴⁾w............ to school, me and my friends. My life ⁽⁵⁾ch............ overnight.
CAROLE	I ⁽⁶⁾w............ to work by car. I talked to two friends who live near me and we ⁽⁷⁾d............ to share a taxi.
ALEK	I always ⁽⁸⁾w............ to college by train. Then I ⁽⁹⁾ch............ my mind about it because the council introduced a new bike service.

b 🔊 7.8 Listen and check.

2 a Look at the sentences in 1a again. Which verbs are
1 talking about a past habit?
2 talking about a specific event in the past?

b Look at the GRAMMAR PANEL and complete the examples with sentences that are true for you.

3 💬 Work in pairs. Ask and answer the questions.
- How did you travel to school when you were younger?
- How did you get to class today? Do you always come by the same form of transport?

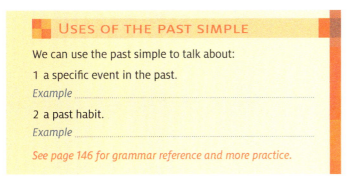

USES OF THE PAST SIMPLE

We can use the past simple to talk about:

1 a specific event in the past.
Example ....

2 a past habit.
Example ....

See page 146 for grammar reference and more practice.

READING & SPEAKING

1 a Read the messages. Match the forms of transport in VOCABULARY 1 to the messages.

1 Getting on the 55 now, c u in 25 mins!

2 Bus late so decided 2 get train. Waiting in station now.

3 We're at arrivals. Where are u? Terminal A or B? Please txt!

4 Arrived 5 mins ago. In cab. Terrible traffic jam ☹! Don't wait 4 me!

5 Just crossing the bridge now. Very windy! Any parking spaces in town?

b 💬 Work in pairs. Answer the questions. Which person
- is waiting to travel?
- is travelling at the moment?
- is at his/her destination already?

2 a Find the text versions of the words in the box in the messages.

you   see you   text   to   minutes   for

b What special text forms do you use in your language?

3 Work in pairs. Read the text messages again. Write them out as full sentences.

4 a 💬 Work in small groups. Choose the best form of transport for each situation. Explain why.
- It's raining. You want to go to the nearest supermarket.
- You and a group of friends want to go camping this weekend in the country.
- You need to go to the capital city of a neighbouring country for a business meeting.

b Compare your answers with the class.

7.4 FUNCTIONAL LANGUAGE: USING PUBLIC TRANSPORT

TUNE IN

1. Match the photos to the places in the box. What are the people doing in each photo?

   ferry terminal   taxi rank   train station
   tourist information   bus stop

2. a 7.9 Listen to five short conversations. Match them to the photos.

   b Listen again and complete the sentences.
   1 She wants to go to the ....
   2 He wants to buy a train ....
   3 He needs to go to terminal .... at the airport.
   4 The .... takes an hour to get to the airport.
   5 The next ferry is in .... minutes.

   "One"
   7.10 Listen to the two questions. Notice the stress on the word before *one*.
   Is there another one?
   When's the next one?
   Listen again and repeat.

FOCUS ON LANGUAGE

3. Read the questions the passengers asked in the conversations. Who are they talking to? Use the people in the box.

   friend (F)   bus driver (BD)   taxi driver (TD)
   tourist information officer (I)   train station worker (TS)

   1 How much is it?
   2 We just missed the last ferry! When's the next one?
   3 Hi! Can you take me to the airport, please?
   4 Excuse me, are you going to the stadium?
   5 Excuse me, how long does it take to get to the airport by train?
   6 Excuse me, this ticket machine is out of order. Is there another one?

4. a Match the answers to the questions in 3.
   a No, you need the number 2 bus.
   b No, I'm afraid there isn't.
   c Yeah, sure. Which terminal?
   d That's £15.85, please.
   e About 35 minutes. There's a train every half an hour.
   f There's another one in 40 minutes.

   b Check your answers in transcript 7.9 on page 165.

OVER TO YOU

5. Look at the photos in 1 again. Act out the five situations.

Speaking task: A programme for a day out

7.5

Tune in

1 💬 Look at the photos. Which places can you find in your town? Which can't you find? Which do you like to go to?

2 a 💬 Work in groups. Think of two things to do, or two places to go, for a visitor to your town who likes
- sports
- art and museums
- music, dancing and cinema
- shopping
- eating good food
- visiting monuments and interesting buildings.

b Work in pairs. Did you do any of these things, or go to any of these places, during the last month? Tell your partner about it.

Prepare for task

3 🔊 7.11 Listen to a tourist guide helping a visitor plan a day out in Lisbon. What kind of things does the visitor want to do? Complete the programme.

Morning
- _____ in the main square.
- Visit the _____.
- Take it easy in the _____ near the castle.

Afternoon
- _____ in the old town.
- Visit the town hall and a _____ exhibition.

Evening
- Go to an open-air theatre in the _____.

4 a Complete the guide's suggestions with the expressions in the box.

| if it's sunny | I suggest | that takes | there's |
| first of all | you can | why not |

1 _____ you can go to the main square.
2 _____ you can sit outside.
3 Then _____ visit the cathedral. _____ about an hour and a half.
4 For lunch, _____ you go to the old town.
5 _____ visit the town hall? _____ a photo exhibition on at the moment.

b 🔊 7.12 Listen and check.

5 Work in pairs. Write questions to ask two other students about what they like doing in their free time. Use the ideas in 2a to help you.

Do you like doing sports? What sports do you like?

6 💬 Work with another pair. Ask your questions and make a note of the answers.

Task

7 Work with your partner in 5. Plan a perfect day out in your town for the students you interviewed in 6. Write notes, using the programme in 3 to help you.

8 Work with your partners in 6. Explain the programme you planned. Are they happy with it?

Report back

9 💬 Tell the class if you were happy with your programme. Why/Why not?

➡ Go to Review C, Unit 7, p. 102   ➡ Go to Writing bank 4, p. 155   **81**

8 IN THE NEWS

1. 💬 Look at the photos of the same place. Answer the questions with a partner.
   - Where is the place?
   - What's happening?
   - Do you think this a good place to watch the news? Why/Why not?

2. Work in pairs to complete A, B and C in the KEY VOCABULARY PANEL 🟩.

3. a 🔊 8.1 Listen to three people answering the questions in A and B. Whose answers are most similar to yours?

   b Listen again and complete the sentences.
   1. Djamal doesn't find out about the news because he...
   2. He thinks most news is...
   3. Jeroen watches the news...
   4. He doesn't like...
   5. Amanda thinks reading the newspaper is...
   6. But she thinks the news in newspapers is too...

82

Key vocabulary

Talking about the news

Sources of news

A How do you find out about the news? Tick the answers in the list.

radio ☐	internet ☐
newspaper ☐	television ☐
mobile phone ☐	podcasts ☐
friends or people at work ☐	

other ....

Types of news

B What kind of news are you interested in? Tick the answers in the list.

sports ☐	local news ☐
national news ☐	world news ☐
business ☐	celebrity gossip ☐
weather ☐	entertainment/culture ☐

other ....

Verb collocations

C Complete the sentences using the verbs in the box. Sometimes more than one option is possible.

listen to   read   watch

1 I usually .... the news *on TV every night at 11 p.m.*
2 I sometimes .... the business news *on the radio in my car.*
3 I often .... the local newspaper *in the bar when I'm having a coffee.*
4 I generally .... the news *on the internet.*
5 I always .... the sports news. *I love football!*

• 💬 Change the words in *italics* so that the sentences are true for you. Compare your sentences with a partner.

NOTICE NEWS OR THE NEWS?

News is uncountable and takes a singular verb:
The news is on TV.

We often use *the* when we talk about news in the media:
I didn't watch the news today.

We can also say *a piece of news* or *some news*:
I have some good news for you.

4 a 💬 Work in small groups. Number these facts about the news in order of agreement (1 = I totally disagree, 5 = I totally agree). Think of examples to support your answers.

- Bad news sells newspapers.
- Gossip and football distract people from real news.
- Nobody reads newspapers. Information is all online.
- The news is different depending on the channel you watch or the newspaper you buy.

b Compare your ideas with the class. Are your answers similar or different?

83

8.1 I MADE THE NEWS

- PRACTISE THE PAST SIMPLE: IRREGULAR VERBS & TIME EXPRESSIONS
- DISCUSS BLOGS & WEBSITES

Reading

1 💬 Work in pairs. Look at the images of blogs above and discuss the questions.
- What is a blog?
- What kind of news do you think these blogs talk about? Which blog would you like to read?
- Do you ever read blogs? If yes, what kind of blogs do you read? If no, why not?

2 a 💬 Work in pairs. Read the headline of the news story below and answer the questions.
1 What do you think the world's oldest blogger wrote about?
2 Would you like to read her blog? Why/Why not?

b Read the article and check your answers.

3 a Read the questions. Can you remember the answers?
1 How old was María Amelia López when she died?
2 Where was she from?
3 When did she start blogging?
4 Why did she start?
5 What did she write about?
6 Why did she enjoy blogging?
7 Who was interested in her blog?
8 Why were they interested?

b Read the article again and check your answers. Why did so many people enjoy her blog?

> **NOTICE** WAS/WERE BORN
> We usually use the past simple with *be born*:
> *When were you born? I was born in 1911.*
> What do you say in your language?

The world's oldest blogger

Before she died in May 2009, María Amelia López, at 97 years old, was the oldest blogger in the world.

This is her first message. She wrote it at the age of 95: 'My name is Amelia and I was born in Muxía, A Coruña, Spain, on 23 December, 1911. Today it's my birthday and my grandson gave me a blog.'

Just before she died, she sat down and wrote: 'When I'm on the internet, I forget about my illness. The distraction is good for you – being able to communicate with people. It's good for the brain, and makes you strong.'

Amelia's blog had more than 1.5 million hits from fans around the world. They read her news and they liked what she said about the world.

She didn't only write about old people's interests. Her blog spoke about everything, from politics and religion, to the power of the internet. She sent a positive message to many people of all ages. She thought life was for living and communicating!

During her life as a blogger, she made a lot of friends and met a lot of celebrities. The day she met the Spanish president, José Luis Rodríguez Zapatero, was an important day for her.

More than 500 readers left messages on her site after her family left a final note from Amelia to the world.

8.1

GRAMMAR

1 Work in pairs. Read the article again. <u>Underline</u> the past simple verbs. Complete 1–13 and a–d in the GRAMMAR PANEL ■ .

2 a Complete the questions with the correct form of the verbs in the box.

> give   be born   make   meet   read   write

1 When _____ she _____ ?
2 Why _____ her grandson _____ her a blog?
3 How long _____ she _____ her blog?
4 _____ a lot of people _____ her blog?
5 _____ she _____ a lot of friends?
6 Which famous politician _____ she _____ ?

b Answer the questions using full sentences.

3 Put the words in the correct order to make sentences in the past simple. Who is the celebrity?

1 born he 1958 was in Chicago in
2 in he 2009 died of 50 at the age
3 Elvis Presley's married he daughter in 1994
4 two children he from a second marriage had
5 his funeral on TV watched 31 million people

4 a Work in groups. Think of a celebrity. Write five sentences about his/her life.

b Read your sentences to the class. Can the other students guess who it is?

■ PAST SIMPLE: IRREGULAR VERBS & TIME EXPRESSIONS

Irregular verbs

Some common verbs have an irregular form in the past simple:

go *went*	meet (4) _____	sit (8) _____
give (1) _____	read (5) _____	speak (9) _____
have *had*	say (6) _____	think (10) _____
leave (2) _____	send (7) _____	write (11) _____
make (3) _____		

In questions and negatives, we use the infinitive:
What did she (12) _____ *about?*
She didn't only (13) _____ *about old people's interests.*

Time expressions

We often use time expressions with the past simple:

> at   during   in   on

(a) _____ 2009   (c) _____ the age of 95
(b) _____ her life   (d) _____ Tuesday

See page 147 for grammar reference and more practice.

PRONUNCIATION: Irregular past simple verbs

1 a Work in pairs. What are the infinitives of the verbs in the box?

> left sat gave spoke read sent met
> said wrote made went had

b))) 8.2 Listen and check.

2 a Complete the table with the past simple of the verbs in 1a.

/əʊ/	/eɪ/	/e/	/æ/
spoke	gave	left	had

b))) 8.3 Listen and check.

LISTENING & SPEAKING

1))) 8.4 Listen to three fans of Amelia's blog. What did they like about it?

2 Listen again. How many of the verbs in GRAMMAR 2a did you hear? Complete the sentences.

1 I _____ Amelia's blog every day.
2 She _____ great advice.
3 She _____ some wonderful things about the past.
4 Her blog really _____ my day.
5 It was wonderful that she _____ the energy to do that.

3 Work in small groups. Discuss the questions.

- Do you have a favourite blog or website?
- Why do you like it?
- How often do you visit it?

8.2 What's it all about?

■ Practise common verbs + the infinitive
■ Discuss news stories & hopes for the future

Speaking & Listening

1 Look at six photos related to three different news stories. Find the words in the box in the photos. Use a dictionary to help you.

> face masks   mud   live concert   soldiers   football fans
> celebrations   passengers   airport   music festival

2 💬 Work in pairs. Discuss the questions.
• What is happening in each photo?
• Which photos go together? There are three pairs. Each pair shows a different story.
• What do you think the stories are about?

3 a 🔊 8.5 Listen to a short news bulletin. Check your answers in 2.

b Listen again and choose the best headline for each story.
1 a Argentinian soldiers fight new flu
   b Flu pandemic in Argentina
2 a Rock festival in danger
   b Singing in the rain
3 a Football heroes come home
   b Fans celebrate league

Vocabulary (1): Lexical sets

1 Work in pairs. Complete the stories with the words in the boxes.

> doctors   hospitals   pandemic   virus

> Fears about the new flu ⁽¹⁾............ are increasing, particularly in inner-city areas. ⁽²⁾............ suspect that 11 soldiers in the Argentinian army have the new ⁽³⁾............ . ⁽⁴⁾............ are on alert in major cities.

> bands   concerts   festival   tickets

> The Rock in the Park ⁽⁵⁾............ is in danger as storms hit Mar del Plata. The organisers cancelled last night's ⁽⁶⁾............ and offered full refunds for ⁽⁷⁾............ . They hope to make an announcement later today about tonight's show with big-name ⁽⁸⁾............ Depeche Mode and The Killers.

2 Read the sports story in transcript 8.5 on page 165. <u>Underline</u> the words associated with football and winning. Then complete the text with the words.

> Lanús won the ⁽¹⁾............ last night for the first time in their history when they ⁽²⁾............ Vélez Sarsfield, 2–0. José Sand ⁽³⁾............ both ⁽⁴⁾............ to give Lanús ⁽⁵⁾............ . Celebrations continued for hours after the ⁽⁶⁾............ .

Speaking & Writing

1 a 💬 Work in pairs. Think of recent news stories from your country. Make notes about what happened.

b Write a short summary of one of the stories. Use the words in Vocabulary (1) 1 and 2 to help you.

2 a Exchange stories with another pair. Write two or three questions asking for more information.

b Exchange questions and write replies.

8.2

Vocabulary (2): Collocations

1 Work in pairs. Identify the noun in each list that you can't use with the verb. Which verb can you use it with?
   1 **get:** the flu, a cold, the league
   2 **go to:** a music festival, the news, a concert
   3 **watch:** a prize, a football match, a film
   4 **win:** a match, a show, a game of cards

2 a Complete the questions with the verbs in 1.
   1 When did you last .... a film on television?
   2 When did you last .... a cold?
   3 When did your local football team last .... a match?
   4 When did you last .... a concert?

   b Ask and answer the questions. Ask more questions to get more information.
   A: *When did you last get a cold?*
   B: *About two weeks ago.*
   A: *Was it bad? Did you go to the doctor?*

Grammar

1 Choose the best subject for each sentence. Which story in SPEAKING & LISTENING 3a does each sentence come from?
   1 Today, the *doctors / authorities* **decided to check** all passengers entering the country's main airports.
   2 The *organisers / news reporters* **hope to make** an announcement later today about tonight's show.
   3 The *club / team* **plans to organise** an official party.
   4 The *club / fans* **want to welcome** the team home.
   5 The *town / team* **would like to thank** their fans.

2 Look at the verbs in **bold** in the sentences in 1. Complete the list of verbs in the GRAMMAR PANEL.

3 a Complete the sentences with the correct form of the verbs *get, go, see* or *stay*.
   1 **I want** .... camping this weekend.
   2 **I'd really like** .... a good film this evening.
   3 **Next summer I plan** .... on holiday to an English speaking country.
   4 **Last weekend I decided** .... at home and study.
   5 **I hope** .... a job with the local TV station.

   b Write sentences about you using the words and phrases in **bold**. Compare your sentences with a partner.

> ### VERB + TO + INFINITIVE
> Some common verbs are always followed by *to* + infinitive.
> Here is a list: decide, ...
> *We want to help you.*
> *They planned to escape.*
>
> See page 147 for grammar reference and more practice.

Listening & Speaking

1 🔊 8.6 Listen to three young people explaining their hopes and plans for the future. Match them to the photos.

2 a Work in pairs. Talk about your hopes and plans for the future.
I plan to study abroad. I'd like to get a new job...

   b Do you have similar hopes or plans? Explain the similarities or differences to the class.

87

8.3 EYEWITNESS ACCOUNTS

- PRACTISE TIME SEQUENCERS
- UNDERSTAND & RETELL A NEWS STORY

AUSTRALIAN POLICE ARREST FRENCH SPIDER-MAN ON SYDNEY SKYSCRAPER

SYDNEY police arrested Alain Robert, 44, also known as the Human Spider, as he climbed the 41-floor Royal Bank of Scotland (RBS) tower in Sydney. He didn't use any ropes or safety equipment and climbed in a strong wind.

A TV cameraman filmed his climb from a helicopter for a documentary programme. Hundreds of people stopped to look as he climbed the tower.

After he finished the climb, police officers took him to the police station, where Robert paid a fine of 200 Australian dollars. This was the Human Spider's eightieth 'free climb' (climbing without ropes), and his third in Sydney.

Robert first climbed a building at the age of 12 when he got locked out of his apartment and decided to climb up eight floors to an open window.

Reading

1 Read the headline and look at the photos. Put them in the order you think they happened.

2 Read the article and check your answers in 1.

3 Read the article again and complete the sentences using the words in the box.

> building   started   filmed   fine
> ropes   top   TV programme

1 Alain Robert didn't have any .... with him on the climb.
2 He climbed to the .... of the RBS tower before the police arrested him.
3 A TV company .... the climb for a ....
4 The police gave Robert a .... of 200 Australian dollars.
5 This was not the first time he climbed a tall ....
6 He was very young when he .... climbing buildings.

4 Read the tweets (Twitter messages) sent by eyewitnesses who watched the Human Spider as he climbed the tower. <u>Underline</u> information which is different from the information in the article.

twitter

> He's climbing up there now, dressed as Spider-Man. It's incredible, the tower is 410 metres high at least!

> A helicopter is flying over him, it's the police, they're going to arrest him.

> He's crazy, kids – do not imitate this!!!

> I'm watching the Human Spider, but he's having trouble, I think he's going to fall... Oh no, he's falling!

5 💬 Work in pairs. Read the article and the tweets again. Which do you think is/are more interesting? Why?

88

Grammar

1 Work in pairs. Put the events in order. (Not all the information appears in the newspaper article.)
1 He got to the top of the tower.
2 They took him to the police station.
3 They arrested him.
4 People stopped to watch him.
5 He started climbing the tower.
6 A helicopter arrived.
7 They found out the helicopter was from a TV company.
8 They asked for his ID.

2 8.7 Listen to an interview with one of the people watching the climb. Check your answers in 1.

3 Listen again. Complete the transcript with the sequencers in the box.

finally   first   then (x2)   later   in the end

> We just didn't believe it! Was that a man on the RBS tower? Was it possible? More and more people stopped to watch. _____ we saw a helicopter. It flew over the tower. We thought it was the police, but they started filming the man on the tower. _____ I found out it was a TV company. We watched him as he climbed higher and higher. _____ he got to the top. It was fantastic, we all cheered! When he came back down the police were there. _____ they asked for his ID, _____ they arrested him and took him away in a police car. I think, _____, they gave him a fine and let him go.

4 Complete 1–4 in the GRAMMAR PANEL.

5 a Work in pairs. Complete the text using some of the sequencers in 3.

> Yesterday was a long day. _____ I had an interview in the morning, _____ I went to work. In the evening I met some friends for a drink and _____ we decided to go to a restaurant for something to eat. _____ we went to a club and I missed my last train! _____ I got home at 3 a.m. and _____ I went to bed at about 4 a.m.

b Tell your partner what you did yesterday. Use as many sequencers as you can.

SEQUENCERS

We use sequencers to show the order of events and actions in a story.
We use (1) _____ to introduce the initial event or action in a series.
We use (2) _____ to introduce the events or actions that follow.
We use (3) _____ to explain that an event or action happened some time after the others.
We use *finally* or (4) _____ to talk about the end of the story.

See page 147 for grammar reference and more practice.

Listening

1 8.8 Listen to a short radio report about Alain Robert. Which of the topics below does the reporter **not** talk about?
1 the beginning
2 the accidents
3 his family
4 the arrests
5 his future plans
6 the reasons why he climbs

2 a Listen again. Make notes about each topic. Which building in the photos does the reporter mention twice?

a The National Bank of Abu Dhabi
b The Eiffel Tower, Paris
c The Lloyd's Building, London
d The Sydney Opera House

b Work in pairs. Compare your notes. Check your answers in transcript 8.8 on page 165.

3 Work in small groups. Retell the story of Alain Robert from memory. Then discuss the questions.
- Do you think Alain Robert is very brave or just crazy? Why?
- Are there any buildings near where you live that you think Alain would like to climb?

8.4 FUNCTIONAL LANGUAGE: RESPONDING TO NEWS

TUNE IN

1. Work in pairs. Look at the photos. What's the news?

2. a 8.9 Listen and check your answers in 1. Match the photos to the conversations.

   b Listen again and complete the sentences.
   1. José and Beth moved into their new house ....
   2. Erika and Kristoff's baby was born ....
   3. Adam lost his job ....
   4. I passed my driving test ....
   5. I can't come to your party ....

3. Did you, or anyone you know, have similar news recently?

FOCUS ON LANGUAGE

4. a Match the responses to the news in 2b.
   a. A girl? That's fantastic news!
   b. Did they? I didn't know it was ready.
   c. Oh, no! What a shame!
   d. That's awful! I'm really sorry to hear that.
   e. That's great news! Congratulations!

   b Check your answers in transcript 8.9 on page 165.

5. a Match the responses in 4a to the notes below.

   Responding to news
   1. Use short questions: *Did you? Was it? Really?*
   2. Use exclamations with **that's** + **adjective**: *That's good (news)!*
   3. Use exclamations with **what** + **a/an** + **noun**: *What a pity! What a great idea!*

   b Look at the responses in 4a again. Which are used for
   1. good news?   2. bad news?

" Responding to news "

 8.10 Listen to the responses in 4a again and mark the main stress in each. Notice how the speakers use exaggerated intonation to show pleasure and sympathy.

Listen again and repeat.

 8.11 Listen to the three responses. Are the speakers really interested?
Oh, what a shame!
Was he?
Really? Well, that's good news!

Repeat the responses. Use the appropriate intonation.

6. 8.12 Listen to the news and respond to it appropriately.

OVER TO YOU

7. Work in pairs. Complete the pieces of news. Make sure that some are good and some are bad.
   1. They *lost / won* the .... last week.
   2. My brother .... his final exam. He's really ....
   3. My parents are hoping to ....
   4. My boyfriend .... the job he really wanted.
   5. Last night I decided not to ....
   6. I'd really like to invite you to ....

8. Change partners. Read your sentences to each other. Respond to the news. Use the language in 4a and 5. Use the appropriate intonation.

90

WRITING TASK: A LOCAL NEWS STORY

TUNE IN

1   Look at the photo. What can you see? What do you think is happening, and where?

2   Read the article and check your answers in 1. Choose the best headline for the article.
   1 Monkeys interrupt official welcome party
   2 Special guests at the mayor's buffet
   3 Thai city celebrates annual monkey buffet

Local news from around the world

More than 2,000 monkeys live in the Thai city of Lopburi. These wild monkeys live happily next to the human population of the city. In fact, the people of Lopburi love their monkey friends so much, they have a party for them at the Prang Sam Yot temple every year. The annual festival takes place on the last weekend in November. It includes a monkey 'tea party'. The people of the city prepare fruit, eggs and cucumbers in their honour. Last year the monkeys ate around 2,000 kilograms of food. The local people believe that giving food to the monkeys brings them good luck.

3   a   Work in pairs. Read the article again and underline the answers to the questions.
   1 Where does the festival take place?
   2 How often does it happen?
   3 When exactly does it take place?
   4 What happens? Why?

   b   Would you like to go and see this festival? Why/Why not?

PREPARE FOR TASK

4   Work in pairs. You are going to read about two more unusual events. Look at the photos. What are the people doing? Why do you think they are doing it?

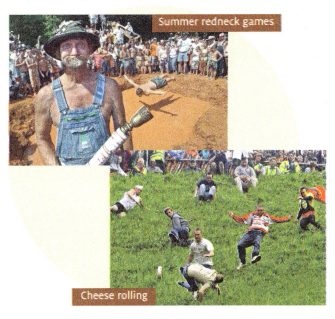

5   a   Student A, turn to page 159. Student B, turn to page 161. Read about the events and answer the questions in 3a.

   b   Tell your partner about the event. Does anything like this ever happen in your town or area?

NOTICE
take place = to happen
take part = to participate

TASK

6   a   Choose a local event that you think seems strange to an outsider. Think about the questions in 3a and make notes about the event.

   b   Read the articles about the events in 2 and 5a again. Make a note of useful language.

7   Write an article or news story about your local event.

REPORT BACK

8   Work in pairs. Read your partner's story. Together decide on a photo and a headline for the story.

9   Share your stories with the class and decide on
   1 the most unusual/interesting story.
   2 the story/photo that tells most about your town.

→ Go to Review C, Unit 8, p. 103

9 HUNGRY PLANET

1 Work in pairs. Look at the photo. What do you think it shows?
   1 the food a family of five people eat in one week
   2 an example of a healthy, balanced diet
   3 the food an average family wastes every month

2 💬 Check your answer on page 161. Are you surprised? Why/Why not? Do you think this is true in your country as well?

3 Look at the word box in the KEY VOCABULARY PANEL. Which foods are in the photo?

4 Complete the exercise in the KEY VOCABULARY PANEL.

5 💬 Work in small groups. Answer the questions.
   • How many different foods from the word map did you eat yesterday? When did you eat them?
     I had rice and chicken for lunch.
   • Did you eat or drink anything that isn't in the word map? Do you know how to say it in English? If not, look it up in a dictionary.
     I had 'cereales' for breakfast. I think that's cereal in English.

92

9.0

KEY VOCABULARY

Food & drink

Write the words in the correct category in the word map. Use a dictionary to help you. Some words can go in more than one category.

apples bananas beans beef
biscuits/cookies bread cakes carrots cheese
chicken chocolate coffee eggs fish
fruit juice ham lettuce milk olives onions
oranges pasta peas potatoes red meat
rice salt and pepper sausages sweets
tea tomatoes water yoghurt

Fruit & vegetables
apples

Dairy
cheese

Food

Sweet snacks
biscuits/cookies

Meat & fish
beef

Carbs
bread

Drinks
coffee

Other
salt and pepper

NOTICE *HAVE LUNCH/FOR LUNCH*
We do not usually use **the** with meals:
for lunch, for breakfast, have lunch, have breakfast
NOT *for the lunch, have the lunch.*

- Add two more words to each category. Use a dictionary to help you.

93

9.1 BREAKFAST

- PRACTISE COUNTABLE & UNCOUNTABLE NOUNS
- DISCUSS DIFFERENT BREAKFASTS

a Khao tom soup
b Doughnut and coffee
c Kahvaltı
d Papaya
e Huevos rancheros
f Muesli

LISTENING

1 Work in pairs. Look at the photos and answer the questions.
1 Which foods look sweet and which look savoury?
2 What part of the world do you think the breakfasts come from? What makes you think that?

I think breakfast b is from the USA because Americans eat a lot of doughnuts.

2 9.1 Listen to a presenter on a TV show talking about breakfasts around the world. Number the photos in the order you hear them.

3 a Listen again and complete the table.

	Country	Key words
1	All over the world	a doughnut, a coffee
2		
3		
4		
5		
6		

b Work in pairs. Check your answers in **1**. Is each breakfast sweet or savoury?

4 Complete the extracts. Listen again and check.
1 In Turkey, for example, breakfast consists of ...., ... and olives, with a cup of .... and maybe some .... and cucumber, or a boiled ....
2 A traditional Brazilian breakfast consists of different .... with fresh .... – papaya, pineapple or melon, for example.
3 Fruit is also very popular in Scandinavia – in Sweden or Norway people often have fruit with .... – usually muesli served with .... Another very healthy choice!
4 In Thailand people start the day with soup – soup with rice and some .... or ....

5 Work in pairs. Which breakfast do you think is
1 the most filling?
2 the best for your health?
3 the most similar to a typical breakfast in your country?

94

9.1

NOTICE *A TOMATO/MILK*

Countable nouns – you can count them:
one tomato, two tomatoes.

Uncountable nouns – they have no plural, you can't count them: *milk* NOT ~~*one milk, two milks*~~.

GRAMMAR

1 Work in pairs. Look at the food words in LISTENING 4.
1 Which are countable?
2 Which are uncountable?
3 Which are used with *a* or *an*?
4 Which are used with *some*?

2 Choose the correct option(s) to complete 1–5 in the GRAMMAR PANEL.

3 Look at the words in the box. Are they countable or uncountable in your language?

> spaghetti   rice   toast   soup   coffee
> tea   meat   fish   fruit   food   wine

4 a Match the words in 3 to the expressions. Use a dictionary to help you. Some words can go with more than one expression.

a bowl of _____
a piece of _____
a slice of _____
a glass of _____
a cup of _____

b Think of one more item of food or drink for each expression.

5 a Complete the sentences with the correct option.
1 I don't have a very healthy diet – I don't really like *fruit / fruits* very much.
2 But I love dairy products – I always have *a / some* milk in the fridge at home.
3 And I really like sweet foods, too, especially cakes and *a biscuits / biscuits*.
4 I don't eat *egg / eggs* very often – I don't like the taste.
5 I prefer to cook *a / some* pasta for a quick meal.

b Rewrite the sentences so that they are true for you.

COUNTABLE & UNCOUNTABLE NOUNS

Countable nouns
a boiled egg, a cake or some biscuits
Countable nouns [1] *can / can't* be plural.
We use *a/an* with [2] *singular / plural* countable nouns.

Uncountable nouns
some toast with butter and jam
We [3] *can / can't* use *a/an* with uncountable nouns.
We [4] *can / can't* use numbers with uncountable nouns.

Some
some tomatoes and a boiled egg
some meat or fish
We can use *some* with [5] *uncountable nouns / singular countable nouns / plural countable nouns*.

See page 148 for grammar reference and more practice.

SPEAKING

1 Read the questionnaire and answer the questions.

> 1 What do you usually have for breakfast?
> 2 What did you have today?
> 3 Do you usually have breakfast
>   a at home?
>   b in a café on your way to work or class?
>   c on the go (you buy something to take away)?
> 4 Do you have the same thing for breakfast at the weekend?

2 a Interview other students in your class. Make a note of their answers.

b Work in pairs. Compare your answers. Write four sentences about your results. Use the language below to help you.

Most people have/had…
Some people have/had…
Others have/had…
Nobody has/had…

3 Share your results with the rest of the class. Do they agree?

95

9.2 PASTA

■ PRACTISE QUANTIFIERS
■ DISCUSS FOOD & EATING HABITS

SPEAKING & READING

1 💬 Work in pairs. Discuss the questions.
   • Do you eat a lot of pasta in your family?
   • What kind of pasta do you usually eat?
   • When did you last eat it?
   • What did you eat it with?

2 Read an article about pasta. Match the headings to the paragraphs. There are two extra headings.
   a Different types of pasta
   b Pasta: a world food
   c Where to find a pasta restaurant
   d How to cook perfect pasta
   e Pasta in Italy

3 Read the article again and answer the questions.
   1 How much pasta does the average Italian eat per year?
   2 Why is pasta popular?
   3 How many different types of pasta are there?
   4 How can pasta be educational?
   5 How does the writer like his/her pasta?
   6 Does the writer think it's easy or difficult to make pasta?

4 a Work in pairs. Read the sentences. What does *it* refer to?

   *And **it** is equally popular in a lot of other countries. It's tasty, it's filling and it's quick and easy to make.*

   b Circle all the examples of *it* in the article. Which examples **don't** refer to pasta?

[1] Pasta is one of the most popular foods in the world. The Chinese ate a type of pasta called noodles 3,000 years ago. The Italian explorer, Marco Polo, introduced noodles to Europe in the thirteenth century. Pasta is now an essential part of Italian culture. Each Italian eats an average of 28 kilograms of pasta a year. And it is equally popular in a lot of other countries. It's tasty, it's filling, and it's quick and easy to make.

[2] Did you know that there are more than 350 different kinds of pasta shapes? You can buy pasta in almost any shape you can imagine. A lot of children even learn to write their first words with a plate of alphabet pasta! And you can serve it with all kinds of sauces: a spicy tomato sauce with a few olives, or a creamy sauce with cheese. Some people eat it with chocolate!

[3] My favourite pasta sauce? It's very simple – olive oil, some black pepper and a little fresh Parmesan cheese, but not too much. And to make perfect pasta? Well, it depends on what kind of pasta you're cooking. It doesn't take much time at all – around seven or eight minutes is usually the ideal cooking time. Make sure that you have lots of water and that it is boiling when you add the pasta. Taste it before you serve it to make sure that it is *al dente* (still a little hard in the middle). You can't go wrong!

Grammar

1 Work in pairs. Read the phrases, a–h. Which include
   1 a countable noun?
   2 an uncountable noun?

   a How much pasta?
   b How many different types of pasta?
   c a lot of children
   d a few olives
   e a little fresh Parmesan cheese
   f too much cheese
   g some black pepper
   h not much time

2 Complete 1–4 and a–d in the GRAMMAR PANEL .

3 a Work in pairs. Complete the questions with *much* or *many*.
   1 How .... coffee do you drink every day? Do you think that's too .... coffee or is it OK?
   2 How .... sweets, cakes or biscuits do you eat in a week? Do you think that's too .... ?
   3 How .... fruit do you eat? And how .... vegetables?
   4 How .... water do you drink? Or do you prefer to drink soft drinks?

   b 💬 Ask and answer the questions.

4 💬 Write three more questions using *how much?* and *how many?* Ask and answer with the rest of the class.

Speaking

1 You are going to interview your classmates about their eating habits. Think of four or five questions to ask about
   • things they like/don't like to eat or drink
   • what time they eat
   • where they eat and who they eat with
   • snacks and eating between meals
   • favourite foods.

   Do you like…? Do you prefer… or…?
   When/Where/Who do you usually…?
   Do you ever…?

2 💬 Ask as many people as you can. Who has the most similar eating habits to you? Tell the rest of the class.
   We both love spicy food. We both usually eat at home with our families. And we both love eating between meals.

QUANTIFIERS
Questions with *how much?* & *how many?*

how much?   how many?

Uncountable nouns

too much   a lot of

some   not much

1 part but not all ....
2 a large quantity ....
3 a small quantity ....
4 more than you need or want ....

Countable nouns

| too many | a lot of | some | a few/not many |

a ....   c ....

b ....   d ....

See page 148 for grammar reference and more practice.

9.3 LOVE FOOD, HATE WASTE

■ Talk about different types of food
■ Discuss alternatives to wasting food

Listening & Reading

1 a Look at the advert. What is its message?
  1 Buy only organic fruit.
  2 Buy local fruit.
  3 Don't waste food.

  b Look at the image on page 159 and check your answer.

2 Work in small groups. Discuss the questions.
  1 Why do people throw food away?
  2 What kind of food do people throw away most?

3 9.2 Listen to someone explaining the advert. Check your answers in 2.

4 a Listen again and complete the extracts.
  1 It's sad but _____ .
  2 That's _____ . _____ million tonnes of food.
  3 Fruit and vegetables are _____ % of this.
  4 The top five fruit and vegetables that go in the rubbish bin are _____ , potatoes, _____ , tomatoes and _____ .
  5 We buy _____ food.
  6 Lots of people forget to put food in the _____ in summer.
  7 If you put fresh fruit and _____ in the fridge, they stay fresh for longer.

  b Check your answers in transcript 9.2 on pages 165–166.

5 Work in pairs. Discuss the questions.
  1 Do you think the facts you heard are true for your country, too? Why/Why not?
  2 What can we do to waste less food? Think of at least three ideas.

6 a Compare your ideas in 5 to the ideas in the list.
  1 Don't cook too much food – think about measurements, e.g. 120 grams of pasta per person.
  2 Don't buy too much food – look at the sell-by dates on food and plan your shop.
  3 Use leftovers (the food you leave on your plate at the end of a meal) for the next meal – use vegetables to make soups, or fruit to make juice.
  4 Cook once, eat twice.

  b Match the advice to the photos.

7 a Read the opinions and match them to the advice in 6a.

I don't like throwing food away. I try to measure food carefully and never cook more than I need.

I love inventing new ways of using leftovers. I use them to make a sauce, or put them in a sandwich.

When I cook I always make enough for two meals. That way I don't have to cook the next day!

I always buy more than I need. Going to the supermarket is a temptation. I try to make a list and keep to that!

  b Do you do any of these things in your family?

Speaking

1 💬 Work in pairs. Match the photos to the food items. Do you usually eat each item or throw it away?

1 a piece of old pizza
2 a very ripe banana
3 leftover spaghetti
4 some dry bread
5 breakfast cereal past its sell-by date

2 💬 Think of some other food items and ask your partner's opinions.

Pronunciation: /ʌ/, /ʊ/, /uː/

1 🔊 9.3 Listen to the sentence. Notice the pronunciation of the vowels in **bold**.

I l**o**ve g**oo**d f**oo**d.

2 🔊 9.4 Listen and repeat the three words.
love /ʌ/   good /ʊ/   food /uː/

3 a Look at the words in the box. Match them to the vowel sounds in **2**.

choose   cook   fruit   look   much   put   soup   too

b 🔊 9.5 Listen and check.

4 a 🔊 9.6 Listen and complete the sentences with six of the words in **3a**.

1 _____ is good for you.
2 I love cold _____.
3 I always _____ fresh _____.
4 People buy _____ food.
5 _____ fresh _____ in the fridge.

b 💬 Rewrite the sentences so that they are true for you. Compare your sentences with a partner.

Vocabulary: Talking about food

1 a Work in pairs. Add the food items in the box to the diagram. Some food can go in more than one category.

~~beans~~   burger   chips   fish   fruit   ice cream
peas   pizza   ready meals   salad   sandwich
vegetables

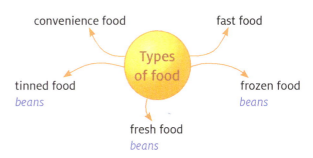

b Add one more word to each category. What type of food do you eat more of?

2 a Use vowels to complete the verbs in the diagram.

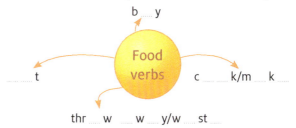

b Complete the questions with the verbs.

1 Do you ever _____ takeaway food to eat at home? If yes, what kinds of food do you _____?
2 Do you ever _____ at your desk when you're working or studying? If yes, what do you usually _____?
3 How often do you _____ food at home? What kinds of food do you usually _____?
4 If you have food on your plate at the end of a meal do you _____ it _____ or keep it for later?

3 💬 Work in small groups. Answer the questions.

9.4 FUNCTIONAL LANGUAGE: EATING OUT

TUNE IN

1 　Work in pairs. Read the menu and discuss the questions.
   1 What kind of restaurant is it?
   2 Are there any restaurants like this in your town?
   3 Why are these restaurants so popular?

2 　What would you like to eat at this restaurant?

I think I'd like a starter and a main course.
I'd like a cheeseburger.

3 a 　9.7 Listen to two friends, Owen and Sofia, ordering a meal from the menu. Complete the table with what they order.

	Owen	Sofia
Starter		
Main course		
Dessert		

b Was their order similar to yours?

FOCUS ON LANGUAGE

4 a Work in pairs. Mark the extracts Owen/Sofia (OS) or waiter (W).
   1 Can we have a table for two?
   2 Are you ready to order?
   3 Can I have the mozzarella and tomato salad, please?
   4 Can I get you something to drink?
   5 Some water for me, please.
   6 Still or sparkling?
   7 Would you like to see the dessert menu?
   8 I'd like the brownie, please.
   9 Can we have the bill, please?
   10 Can I pay by card?

b 　9.8 Listen and check.

> **Intonation**
> Listen again to the sentences in 4a. Do the speakers' voices go up ↗ or down ↘?
> Practise repeating the sentences using the correct intonation.

The Gourmet Burger Bar

Starters

Mozzarella and tomato salad
The finest mozzarella and beef tomatoes with fresh basil, pesto and extra virgin olive oil.

Chicken wings
Barbecued chicken wings served with homemade mayonnaise and green jalapeño peppers.

Burgers – Today's Specials

Habanero cheeseburger
100% organic beef, mozzarella cheese, hot and spicy sauce, salad and mayonnaise.

Veggie
Vegetarian burger, aubergine, goat's cheese and mixed-leaf salad.

Italian chicken
Organic chicken burger, avocado, pesto sauce and salad.

Desserts

Chocolate brownie and ice cream
Freshly baked brownie served with vanilla ice cream.

Fruit of the day
Fresh strawberries topped with a blend of honey and fresh yoghurt.

OVER TO YOU

5 　Work in groups of three. Student A, you are the waiter. Students B and C, you are the customers. Act out the scene.

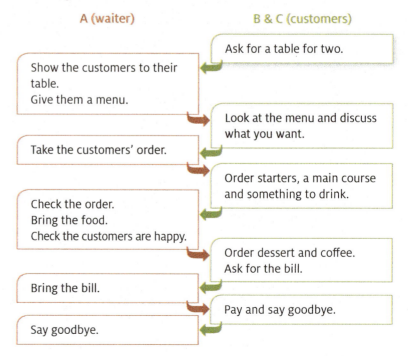

A (waiter) / B & C (customers)

- Ask for a table for two.
- Show the customers to their table. Give them a menu.
- Look at the menu and discuss what you want.
- Take the customers' order.
- Order starters, a main course and something to drink.
- Check the order. Bring the food. Check the customers are happy.
- Order dessert and coffee. Ask for the bill.
- Bring the bill.
- Pay and say goodbye.
- Say goodbye.

6 　Change roles. Turn to page 160 for a new restaurant and menu.

Speaking task: A description of a meal

9.5

Tune in

1 🗨 Look at the photos. How often do you eat like this?

2 a Read the sentences. Which are true for you?
- I eat out most days.
- I often eat out at weekends.
- I love eating out with friends.
- I only eat out on special occasions.
- I prefer to eat at home.

b 🗨 Work in pairs. Compare your answers. Then discuss the questions.
1 When did you last eat out?
2 Where did you go?
3 Who did you go with?

Prepare for task

3 🔊 9.9 Listen to Owen talking about his meal with another friend. Which of the adjectives in the box does he use? Is his general opinion positive or negative?

> busy   convenient   delicious   expensive   fast
> good   great   original   relaxed   slow

4 Listen again. Match the adjectives to the features.
1 the location (just round the corner)
2 you don't have to book
3 the atmosphere
4 the food
5 the menu
6 the burger
7 the service

5 Think about a bar, restaurant or café that you went to recently. Make notes about
- the place itself: pleasant/awful, old-fashioned/modern?
- the atmosphere: relaxed/formal?
- the food: boring/tasty, excellent/OK?
- the menu: varied, interesting, original?
- the staff: friendly/unfriendly?
- the service: fast/slow?
- the price: cheap/expensive?
- anything else: location, music, decor?

Task

6 🗨 Work in small groups. Talk about the restaurants you visited. Write your answers in the table below. Use the key.

7 🗨 Work in pairs. Decide which place is best for
1 a business lunch or meeting.
2 a birthday party for a friend.
3 an evening out with your family.

Report back

8 🗨 Discuss your decisions with the class.

Name of student	Name of restaurant	Location	Food	Atmosphere	Price
1					
2					
3					
4					

★★★★ out of this world   ★★★ very good   ★★ average   ★ don't go!

→ Go to Review C, Unit 9, p. 104   → Go to Writing bank 5, p. 156

Review C Unit 7

Vocabulary
The weather

1 a Complete the weather nouns with vowels.

s..n   f..g   ..c..
w..nd   sn..w   cl..d

b Transform them into adjectives.

2 Work in pairs. Discuss the questions.
1. What's the weather like now?
2. What was it like yesterday?
3. What's the weather usually like in your town in autumn, winter, spring and summer?
4. What do you do in extreme weather – when it's really hot, cold, rainy, etc.?

Transport

3 a Rank the forms of transport in order of preference (1–7) for use in your town.

| motorbike | car | bike | bus | train | subway | taxi |

b Work in pairs. Discuss the questions.
1. Which form of transport do you usually use?
2. Which did you use today?
3. How was your journey? How long did it take?

4 R11 Listen to Paul and Barbara discussing transport in Lyon. Mark the statements true (T) or false (F).

1. Paul says the new bike service is really cheap.
2. Barbara believes bikes and scooters are equally popular.
3. Paul says that people drive cars a lot because of the weather.
4. The price of petrol is expensive at the moment.

5 What transport culture does your town/city have? Do people travel by car, scooter, bike or public transport? Why?

Public transport is slow here because the traffic is bad, but it's cheap.

Grammar
Past simple

1 Work in pairs. Think about the first time you did something. What did you do? When was it? Where were you? Who was with you? Did you like the experience?

The first time I went abroad: It was four years ago – I went to Greece with my family. It was our summer holiday. I had a great time!

2 a Write the past simple form of the verbs.

decide .... do .... go .... travel ....
stop ....   have .... wait .... stay ....

b Write a paragraph about a recent trip. Try to use as many of the verbs as possible.

3 Work in pairs. Ask your partner about his/her trip. Was it similar or different to yours?

Functional language
Using public transport

1 Write the words in the correct order.
1. next When bus is to city centre the the ?
2. you me take the to Can please train station ?
3. long How take get to to does the cathedral it ?
4. train this Does go the park to ?

2 a Read the questions again. Where are the people who are asking the questions? Who are they asking?

b Work in pairs. Continue the conversations.

▶ Looking back

- Tell a partner what you did last weekend.
- Can you remember what the weather was like every day last week?
- Think of five things you did regularly when you were 10 years old. Compare your answers with a partner.

Unit 8

REVIEW C

Vocabulary

Talking about the news

1 Work in pairs. Think of five different types of news, e.g. sports.

Which are you

1 always interested in?
2 sometimes interested in, it depends on the stories?
3 never interested in? Why?

2 Discuss the questions.

1 What is the main story in the news today?
2 Did you know about this story before, or was it new to you?
3 How did you find out about it?
4 Would you like to know more about it?
5 How can you find out more?

Lexical sets

3 a Look at the groups of words. Which word in each group is not part of that lexical set?

1 doctor pandemic hospital ticket
2 concert alert festival band
3 goal virus victory score

b Work in pairs. Match the lexical sets in **a** to the types of news.

a entertainment   b health   c sports

4 Think of three words to add to each lexical set. Then think of a story for each set. Take it in turns to tell your partner as much as you can about the stories.

Collocations

5 a Complete the questions.

1 Do you ever .... music festivals? Are there any big festivals in your area? When and where do they take place? Do you usually go? Why/Why not?
2 Did your country .... any medals in the last Olympics? Which sports is your country famous for? Do you play any of them?
3 What type of film do you usually .... ? What's your favourite film? Why?
4 Do you often .... colds? What do you usually do to help you feel better?

b Choose one of the groups of questions in **a**. Discuss them with a partner.

Grammar

Past simple: irregular verbs

1 Write the verbs in the past simple.

1 I .... (write) about 20 text messages yesterday.
2 I .... (read) the news headlines on the internet this morning.
3 I .... (send) my friend an email for her birthday.
4 I .... (meet) my friends for a coffee.
5 I .... (speak) to my boss about a problem at work.
6 I .... (make) a mistake in my English homework.

2 Are the sentences true for you? If not, write sentences with the same verbs that are true for you. Compare your answers with a partner.

Sequencers

3 a Look at the actions. Which did you do this morning?

read the newspaper   have a coffee   get a bus
listen to the radio   have a shower   call a friend
go shopping   go to work   go to class

b What order did you do them in? Tell a partner. Use sequencers to explain the order.

4 Were your mornings similar or very different?

Functional language

Responding to news

1 R12 Listen to some people announcing some news. Choose the best response in the box to each piece of news.

Did they? When?   Did she? I didn't know that!
Oh, that's great news!   Oh no! What a shame!

2 Work in pairs. Student A, turn to page 160. Student B, turn to page 161. Take it in turns to respond to your partner's news.

■ Looking back

- What's the most memorable news story in this unit? Why?
- What good news and bad news did you have recently? Can you describe what the news was?
- How many irregular past simple verbs can you now use? How can you remember them?

Unit 9

Vocabulary
Food & drink

1 **a** Work in pairs. Look at the food pyramid. How many foods can you name in two minutes?

  b 💬 Discuss the questions.
  - Which are your favourite foods?
  - Are there any foods you don't like or can't eat?

2 **a** Match the words to the categories.

   1 verbs   a spicy, sweet, filling, ...
   2 measuring food and drink   b a bowl of, a slice of, a piece of, ...
   3 types of food   c eat, cook, waste, ...
   4 adjectives to describe food   d fast, fresh, tinned, ...

  b Add one more word to each category. Then think of two more categories and four words for each one.

Grammar
Countable & uncountable nouns

1 Underline the correct words to complete the descriptions.

   Breakfast
   I had (1)*a coffee / some coffees* and (2)*a slice / some slice* of toast with (3)*a / ø* butter and (4)*honey / honeys*.

   Lunch
   I had some (5)*salad / salads*, (6)*a / a bowl of* soup and some (7)*bread / breads*.

   Evening meal
   I had (8)*spaghetti / spaghettis* with (9)*a / some* seafood and a glass of (10)*wine / some wines*.

2 💬 Write descriptions of what you had to eat yesterday. Compare your descriptions with a partner.

Quantifiers

3 Complete the questions using *much* or *many*.

   1 How .... fruit did you eat yesterday?
   2 How .... different vegetables did you eat?
   3 How .... cups of coffee did you have?
   4 How .... water did you drink?

4 💬 Work in pairs. Ask and answer the questions in 3. Who has the healthiest diet? You or your partner?

Functional language
Eating out

1 Order the phrases to form short dialogues.

   1 a Certainly. Come with me.
      b Yes, can we have a table for two, please?
      c Are you waiting for a table?
   2 a Yes, the buffet for me, please.
      b A house salad, please.
      c And for you, sir?
      d Are you ready to order?
   3 a And some water, please.
      b Sparkling, please.
      c Can we have two beers, please?
      d Can I get you something to drink?
      e Still or sparkling?
   4 a Yes, thanks. Can we have the bill, please?
      b Is everything OK?
      c Certainly. Just a moment.
   5 a Can I pay by card?
      b Thank you.
      c OK, here you are.
      d I'm sorry, we only accept cash.

2 **a** 🔊 R13 Listen and check.

  b 💬 Practise the dialogues in groups of three.

3 Use adjectives to complete the email.

> We went to that new restaurant I told you about yesterday. It was really .... It's very .... , just two doors down from the office. The food is .... It's quite simple, but really fresh. And the staff are very .... We must go there together next time you're in town.
> P x

🟧 Looking back

- Think of five questions you can ask about food and eating.
- Think of five things you can say about your eating habits.
- What other foods would you like to know the name of in English?
- Can you describe your favourite meal?

104

BRING IT TOGETHER 7, 8 & 9

REVIEW C

LISTENING

1 🔊 **R14** Listen to Ruth talking about her language learning experiences. Answer the questions.
   1 What two languages does she talk about?
   2 Where did she learn the first one?
   3 And the second one?
   4 What did she enjoy most about learning the second language?

2 **a** Listen again. Match the statements to the two languages.
   1 I can communicate in simple situations.
   2 Reading really helps me to learn.
   3 I passed all my exams.
   4 We did a lot of speaking.
   5 We did a lot of translating.
   6 We played a lot of language games.

   b 💬 Are any of the statements in 2a true about your language learning experiences? Compare your answers with a partner.

SPEAKING

3 **a** 💬 Work in pairs. Order the activities from 1 to 6 (1 = most important, 6 = least important).
   ☐ learning about grammar and pronunciation
   ☐ speaking with correction
   ☐ speaking with no correction
   ☐ listening to real conversations
   ☐ reading books or articles in English
   ☐ writing short texts and messages in English

   b Compare your answers with the rest of the class.

4 **a** Think about five different kinds of activities you did in class in the last three units.

   b 💬 Show your list to a partner and answer the questions. Compare your ideas with the rest of the class.
   1 Which activity helped you most? Why?
   2 Which activity did you enjoy most? Why?
   3 What kind of activities would you like to do more of in the next three units?

QUICK CHECK

Complete the checklist below.

Can you...	Yes, I can.	Yes, more or less.	I need to look again.
1 talk about what happened in the past?	☐	☐	☐
2 talk about the weather?	☐	☐	☐
3 discuss forms of transport?	☐	☐	☐
4 talk about the news?	☐	☐	☐
5 respond to news?	☐	☐	☐
6 talk about food and your eating habits?	☐	☐	☐
7 order a meal in a restaurant?	☐	☐	☐
8 describe a meal?	☐	☐	☐

💬 Compare your answers with a partner.
- What else do you know now after studying units 7–9?
- Do you need to look again at any of the sections?
- Do you need any extra help from your teacher?

105

10 STATE OF THE ART

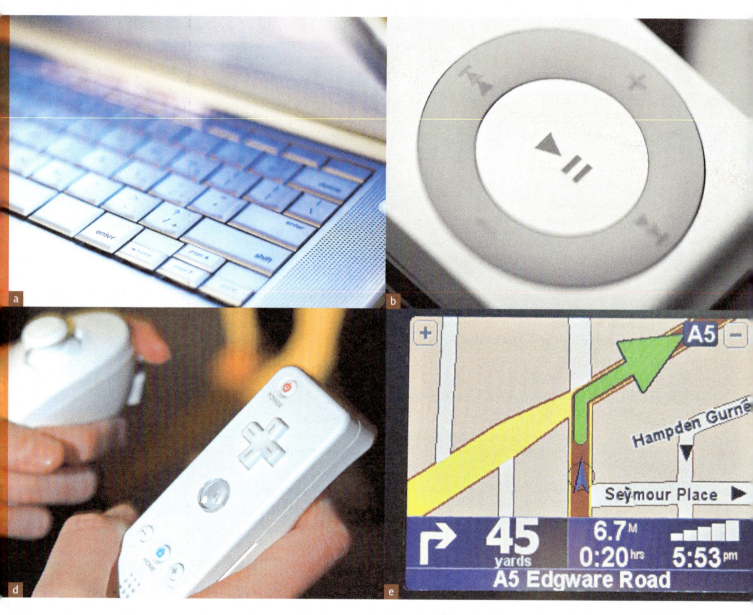

1 a Work in pairs to complete A in the KEY VOCABULARY PANEL.

b 💬 Discuss the questions.
- Which gadgets do you have?
- Which do you use every day?
- Which is your favourite and least favourite? Why?

2 💬 Look again at the list of functions in A. Answer the questions.
- What did people use 30 years ago to do these things?
- Which of these 'old-fashioned' gadgets do you still use, if any?

3 a 🔊 10.1 Listen to two friends. Which of the gadgets are they talking about?

b Listen again and complete B in the KEY VOCABULARY PANEL.

4 🔊 10.2 Look at the adjectives in B again and find seven pairs of opposites. Listen and check.

5 💬 Think of a gadget you have. Which of the adjectives in B can you use to describe it? Tell a partner about it.

I have an old digital camera. It's big and heavy. I'd like to buy a new one – something small and light.

106

10.0

KEY VOCABULARY

Technology

Gadgets

A Match the photos (a–f) to the gadgets.

> computer game   digital camera   satnav
> flatscreen TV   laptop   MP3 player

NOTICE

gadget = a small piece of equipment that does something useful or impressive

- Match the gadgets to the functions. Some gadgets have more than one function.
  1. You can use it to take photos.
  2. You can use it to store information.
  3. You can use it to listen to music.
  4. You can use it to get directions.
  5. You can use it to watch films and video clips.
  6. You can use it to play games.

Adjectives to describe gadgets

B 10.1 Tick the adjectives in the box that you hear.

> heavy   new   difficult   small   good
> light   cheap   quick   bad   old   slow
> expensive   big   easy

Parts of a computer

C Label the computer with the words in the box.

> ~~screen~~   mouse   keyboard   webcam
> DVD drive   speakers   Wi-Fi   memory stick

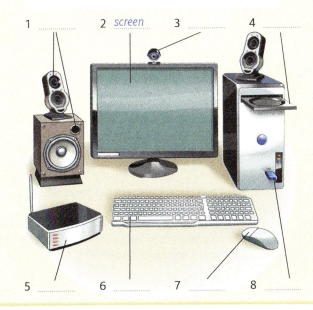

1 ....   2 *screen*   3 ....   4 ....
5 ....   6 ....   7 ....   8 ....

6 Work in pairs to complete **C** in the KEY VOCABULARY PANEL.

7 a Discuss the questions with a partner.
- Do you use a computer?
- What kind of computer do you use (a PC, a laptop, a netbook)?
- What do you use it for?
- Does it have all the features in the picture in **C**?
- Are you happy with it, or would you like a new one? Why?

b Report back to the class.

Marek uses a computer at work and he has a laptop at home. He likes his laptop, it's new. But he wants a new computer at work. It's old and slow.

10.1 MAD ABOUT GADGETS

- PRACTISE COMPARATIVE ADJECTIVES
- COMPARE GADGETS & TALK ABOUT PREFERENCES

LISTENING & SPEAKING

1 a Work in pairs. Look at the photo and discuss the questions.
- What kind of gadget does it show?
- What can it do?

b 10.3 Listen and check.

2 Listen again and complete the description from an online magazine.

PRODUCT REVIEWS

What's different about our new e-reader?

You can store more than .... books on it. You can read your favourite .... , magazines and blogs from the internet. The new, stronger battery gives you a full .... of reading time.

Comments (19)

3 Work in pairs. Think of two advantages and two disadvantages of an e-reader. Compare your answers with the class. Would you like to buy an e-reader? Why/Why not?

Lucia

I have a screen at work. I look at it all day. I don't want another screen for reading. I'm **happier** reading a real book. I like to feel the pages, turn them over – it's **more relaxing**.

Paul

It's definitely **more expensive** than buying normal books. Just think, you can buy maybe 150–200 books for the price of one e-reader! And it's not only the money for the gadget: you need to buy the e-books as well.

Kostis

Paul, imagine carrying 100 books with you everywhere you go! And remember, e-books are **cheaper** than paper books. I love my e-reader! And the new model is even **better** – it's **bigger**, the battery's **stronger**... I'm going to get one as soon as I can!

Kurt

I read the newspaper on my e-reader on the train every morning. It's definitely **better** than the conventional paper – **more comfortable**, **easier**... and it saves trees. This is the future, I think!

READING

1 Read the comments by four people. Does anybody make the same points as you in LISTENING & SPEAKING 3? What other advantages and disadvantages do the people talk about?

2 Read the comments again and answer the questions.
1 Which people are negative and which are positive about the e-reader?
2 Who owns an e-reader already? How do you know?
3 Who wants to buy a new one? How do you know?

3 Work in pairs. Mark the sentences true (T) or false (F).
1 Lucia likes reading e-books on her computer.
2 Paul says the e-reader is expensive.
3 Kostis prefers the old model.
4 Kurt is not very enthusiastic.

Grammar

1 Work in pairs. Look at the words in **bold** in the comments on page 108. Complete 1–7 in the GRAMMAR PANEL.

2 a Complete the sentences using the correct comparative form of the adjectives in brackets.
1 Reading a good book is _____ (relaxing) than watching a TV programme.
2 Digital cameras are _____ (easy) to use than conventional cameras.
3 Advances in technology make our lives _____ (safe) and _____ (happy).

b Do you agree with the sentences? Why/Why not?

3 a Work in pairs. Look at the photos. Write sentences comparing the two models. Use the adjectives in the box.

big   cheap   expensive   fashionable   small

b Which one would you prefer to buy? Why?

4 Work in pairs. Turn to page 160. Look at the pictures and follow the instructions. Compare your answers with the class.

COMPARATIVE ADJECTIVES

We use comparative adjectives to compare and contrast two things:
The e-reader is lighter than a book.

We use the preposition *than* with comparative adjectives:
The old model is heavier than the new one.

Forming comparative adjectives

One syllable: adjective + *-er*
fast → faster   cheap → (1) _____   strong → (2) _____

With some one-syllable adjectives the spelling changes:
big → (3) _____

Two syllables ending in *-y*: change *-y* to *-i* and add *-er*
easy → (4) _____   happy → (5) _____

Two syllables or more: *more* + adjective
expensive → more expensive   comfortable → (6) _____

Irregular adjectives
good → (7) _____   bad → worse

See page 149 for grammar reference and more practice.

Speaking

1 Work in pairs. Look at the gadgets below. Think of two adjectives to describe each gadget. Use a dictionary to help you.

2 a Complete the sentence comparing any two of the gadgets.
This gadget is _____ than the other one.

b Read your sentence to the class. Can they guess which two gadgets you're talking about? Do they agree?

3 Which gadget would you like to get as a birthday present? Why?

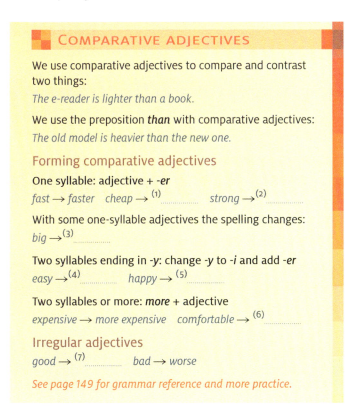
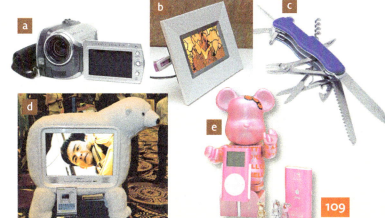

10.2 CONNECTING PEOPLE

- PRACTISE *GOING TO* FOR FUTURE PLANS
- DISCUSS THE USES OF MOBILE PHONES

Speaking

1 a 💬 Work in pairs. Look at the photos. What are the people doing on their phones? Think of three other things you can do with your phone.

b Compare your list with the class. How many functions are there in total? Which do you use most? Why?

I send text messages, it's cheaper.

Notice *mobile or cell?*

Mobile phone is British English, *cell phone* is American English.
We often say *mobile* or *cell* on its own, without *phone*:
Where's my mobile/cell?

2 a 💬 Work in groups. You are going to take part in a survey on mobile phones. Turn to page 161.

b Report the group's answers to the class.

Dimitri's cell phone wakes him up in the morning with the alarm – it's the first thing he sees!

3 a 💬 Work in pairs. Are the items advantages or disadvantages of mobile phones?

- anti-social
- useful in emergencies
- cost
- you are never alone
- people know where you are
- public phones are terrible
- they can easily break

b Can you think of any other advantages or disadvantages? Share your ideas with the class.

Reading

1 Work in pairs. Read the headline of the article below. What mobile phone functions do you think the article will talk about?

2 Read the article and check your answers in **1**. What is each person planning to do with his/her phone?

3 a Read the article again. Which person talks about
1 public information messages? 3 phone rental?
2 money transfer?

b Which programme do you think helps people most?

CELL PHONES FIGHTING POVERTY

Cell phones are changing the lives of millions of people around the world. They are giving them new job opportunities, improved medical conditions and the chance to make plans for the future. Here are a few true stories from people who are just receiving this technology.

Safaricom, Kenya
Samson lives in Nairobi and sends money home to his mother, who lives in the country. The bank system can be slow and very expensive. In the past he often lost money.
'Now I'm going to use my cell phone to send money to my mother. She can text me when the money arrives. It's quicker, safer and easier. Isn't that great?'

Grameen Village Phone Programme, Bangladesh
Hasina bought a phone from the Grameen programme for $110. She pays $2.50 a week to the programme. She rents the phone to people in her village for a small fee.
'I get about $25 a month from the phone. I'm not going to spend all the money. I'm saving it. I'm going to open a small grocery store with the money – I want to give my family some kind of future.'

FrontlineSMS, Malawi
Karen is a volunteer nurse. She works with HIV patients. The nurses have big problems contacting peope who live in remote villages.
'We're going to use the new phones to send text messages to patients with information about medicine and health care. We're going to distribute about 200 cell phones to remote villages. It's great news for rural Malawi.'

GRAMMAR

1 Work in pairs. Read the article again. Match the two halves of the sentences.

1 Samson is going to
2 Hasina isn't going to
3 The nurses are going to
4 The villagers are going to

a distribute 200 phones to remote villages.
b spend all the money she makes.
c send money to his mother.
d share the phones.

2 Underline all the examples of *going to* in the article and **1**. Choose the correct option to complete 1–7 in the GRAMMAR PANEL.

3 Complete the sentences with the correct form of *going to*.

1 It _____ be difficult to start with.
2 We _____ teach two or three people in each village how to use the phone.
3 We _____ limit the use of the phones to medical uses.
4 One man _____ call his daughter.

4 a 10.4 Listen to Karen talking about the project in Malawi and check your answers in **3**.

b Listen again. Why are they going to do the things in **3**?

5 a Write questions using *going to*.

1 you/stay in tonight?
2 you/do any shopping after class?
3 What/you/do next weekend?
4 What/you/do next summer?

b Work in pairs. Ask and answer the questions.

6 Change pairs. Tell your new partner about your previous partner's plans.

GOING TO

We use *be* + *going to* + infinitive to talk about future plans.

+	I (1)'m / 're / 's going to send money to my mother. Hasina (2)'m / 're / 's going to open a grocery store.
–	You (3)'m not / aren't / isn't going to get a new phone.
?	(4)Am / Are / Is they going to distribute new phones? (5)Am / Are / Is she going to spend all the money?
Yes/No	Yes, they (6)am / are / is. No, she (7)'m not / aren't / isn't.

See page 149 for grammar reference and more practice.

PRONUNCIATION: /ɪ əʊ ə/

1 10.5 Listen to the exchange. Notice the pronunciation of *going to*.

/gənə/
A What are you going to do?
/gənə/
B I'm going to wait and see.

2 a 10.6 Listen to four questions. Match them to the answers.

a Youssef and Kelly.
b In the bar.
c Yes, I am.
d I don't know. Go for something to eat, maybe?

b Listen again and repeat the questions.

3 Work in pairs. Talk about your plans for the evening.

111

10.3 GETTING TOGETHER

- PRACTISE PERSONAL PRONOUNS
- DISCUSS DIFFERENT FORMS OF COMMUNICATION

VOCABULARY: Communication

1 Look at the pictures. What's the person doing in each?

2 a Work in pairs. Write the verbs on the correct line. Some verbs can go on both lines.

> ~~answer~~ call back email ~~call~~
> text reply ring phone

contact: *call,* ....
respond: *answer,* ....

b Which verbs do you use
1 for talking on the phone?
2 for communicating by text or email?

3 Work in pairs. Discuss which form of communication in 1 you think is best for the situations.
- You want to wish a friend happy birthday.
- You know you're going to be late getting home.
- You want to discuss a project with a colleague.
- You need to contact your parents overseas.
- You need to organise a meeting with a large group of people.

4 a Work in small groups. Think of three or four other ways we use to communicate with people.

b Match the adjectives in the box to the forms of communication in 1. Then answer the questions.

> fast slow cheap expensive personal
> impersonal easy complicated

- Which do you use regularly?
- Which do you never use? Why?

LISTENING

1 Work in pairs. Match the photos to the captions.

> In memoriam
> It's No Pants Day!
> NY pillow fight
> A silent rave

2 a 💬 Look at the photos again and answer the questions.
1 Where are the people and what are they doing?
2 What do the photos have in common?
3 Which is different? Why?

b 🔊 10.7 Listen to a TV interview about the events in the photos and check your answers.

3 a Listen again. Mark the statements true (T) or false (F). If false, correct them.
1 Flash mobs meet in private.
2 These meetings last a short time.
3 People find out about them from the news.
4 The silent rave happened in New York.
5 The Espanyol fans organised the event by phone and text message.
6 Frederic doesn't have a favourite flash mob.

b 💬 Would you like to take part in a flash mob event? Why/Why not?

Grammar

1 🔊 10.8 Listen to a conversation between two people and answer the questions.

1 What kind of event are they planning?
2 What time is it going to take place?
3 Where are they going to meet?

2 a Work in pairs. Look at the extracts and circle the correct answer.

JON Hi! Did you get the message?
CORINA Yes, but I deleted ⁽¹⁾*it / them* by mistake.

CORINA Did you text Tomas? I know ⁽²⁾*he / him* 's really interested.
JON No, I don't have his number. Can you call ⁽³⁾*he / him*?

CORINA Sure. What about Dan and Carlos? ⁽⁴⁾*They / Them* definitely want to come, too. And Sue. ⁽⁵⁾*She / Her* loved the last one!
JON Oh no, I forgot about ⁽⁶⁾*she / her*.

CORINA What time are ⁽⁷⁾*we / us* going to meet? How many of ⁽⁸⁾*we / us* are going to be there?

JON Bring your pillow, remember! And pass the message on!
CORINA No problem. Let ⁽⁹⁾*I / me* know if there's a change of plan!

b Listen again and check your answers.

3 Work in pairs. Read the GRAMMAR PANEL . Are your answers in 2 subject pronouns or object pronouns? Complete 1–6 in the GRAMMAR PANEL .

4 a Complete the voicemail messages with a subject or object pronoun.

1 Hi! It's Tracey. Nothing urgent, but can you call _____ when you get a minute? Bye!
2 Where are you? It's Adriana and João. Let _____ know where you are. We're worried.
3 Hello. This is a message for Stefano. I spoke to the lawyers. Can you meet _____ tomorrow at ten? Thanks. Let _____ know asap! Bye!
4 Hi. This is Paul. Julie's still waiting for the book. Can you send _____ to _____ soon? Thanks! Bye!

b 🔊 10.9 Listen and check.

PERSONAL PRONOUNS

We use personal pronouns instead of the names of people and things.
Subject pronouns come before the verb:
I'm going to call Tomas.
Object pronouns come after the verb:
I'm going to call him.
We also use object pronouns after prepositions:
Tomas is going to come with us.

Subject	Object
I	(1)
you	you
he	(2)
(3)	her
it	(4)
we	(5)
(6)	them

See page 149 for grammar reference and more practice.

Speaking

1 💬 Work in groups to organise a flash mob in your town. Use the prompts to help you.

• My flash mob is going to be… *(fun/a protest/ something else).*
• It's going to take place in… *(place)* at… *(time).*
• I'm going to tell people via… *(text message, blog, etc.).*
• We're going to do… *(activity)* during the flash mob.
• It's going to last… *(minutes/hours).*

2 💬 Compare your ideas with the class. Are any of the ideas similar? Which do you think is the best event? Why?

10.4 FUNCTIONAL LANGUAGE: GIVING INSTRUCTIONS

British phone users want simpler phones

New phones are more difficult to use and have too many applications that a lot of us are not interested in. Many users are only interested in texting and making calls. Functions like taking photos and listening to music are popular, but not essential. Most of us are more interested in good sound quality, good coverage and, most importantly, checking the time!

However, there's the other extreme – the minority that loves these new applications. Did you know that now you can get a device that allows you to identify birdsong, another that tunes a musical instrument and even one that repels mosquitoes (the phone produces a noise that scares them away)! Can you believe it?

TUNE IN

1 Read a short article about British mobile phone users. Tick the functions mentioned.

   1 making a phone call
   2 sending a text message
   3 receiving email
   4 taking photos
   5 shopping
   6 listening to music
   7 checking the time

2 Read the article again and answer the questions.
   1 What other functions or features does the article talk about?
   2 Which are the most important for British phone users?
   3 Do you think mobile phone users in your country think the same? Why/Why not?

3 a 10.10 Listen to three short conversations. What functions or features do the people talk about?

   b Listen again. What does each person want to do with the phone?

FOCUS ON LANGUAGE

4 a Match the functions to the instructions.

   1 making a call   a Click here – see where it says 'more'?
   2 sending a photo   b Click on 'menu'.
   3 checking the time   c Press that button on the side.
                            d Press the button with the green phone.
                            e Select 'camera'.
                            f Select 'send'.
                            g Key in the number.

   b Listen to 10.10 again and check. Which instructions are introduced using
   1 just?
   2 now?
   3 then?

5 Read transcript 10.10 on page 166. Are the instructions the same for your phone? Show your partner how to do the three functions in 4 on your phone.

> **Checking understanding**
>
> 1 See?   2 Yeah, that's it!   3 Now I get it!
>
> Which person is
> a saying that they now understand the instruction?
> b checking that the other person understands?
> c confirming that the other person is following the instructions correctly?
>
> 10.11 Listen. Does the speaker's voice go up ↗ or down ↘?
>
> Listen again and repeat.

OVER TO YOU

6 Work in pairs. Think of another useful gadget. Write instructions to explain one of its main functions.

7 Read your instructions to the class. Can they guess what the gadget is?

WRITING TASK: A CLASS FORUM

10.5

Internet forums can answer any question!

Do you know the saying, 'two heads are better than one'? Well, imagine how good 100 heads, or 1,000 heads or 100,000 heads can be! This is the idea behind internet forums, where you can ask a question, any question, online and get answers from people all over the world. Some of the answers are good; some of them are not so good. But when there are millions of people ready to answer your questions, sooner or later the answer will be very, very good – if not perfect! We tried it out to see. We posted this simple question and then waited for the answers.

I'm planning a trip to New York City. When is the best time to visit the city? Thanks.

Here are the answers.

1) October. Autumn colours are beautiful in Central Park and it's low season, so it will be cheaper to get a room.
☆☆☆☆☆ Rate the answer.

2) Christmas vacation, wonderful time for all your presents and it might snow! So romantic!
☆☆☆☆☆ Rate the answer.

3) August is the best month – all the New Yorkers go away then and you can have the city to yourself.
☆☆☆☆☆ Rate the answer.

As I said, not all good, but one was exactly what I wanted to know! Guess which one it was.

TUNE IN

1 💬 Work in pairs. Look at the photos and discuss the questions.
- Where are the people?
- What questions do you think they want to ask?
- Who do you think is going to give the answer?
- Do you know someone who can give you the best answer to these questions?
  Which is the best computer to buy?
  Can you recommend a good restaurant?

2 Read the article about internet forums. How can they help you get the right answer to your questions?

NOTICE ANY

You can use *any* with a singular noun in affirmative sentences to show that there is no limit to the possibilities:

any question = all possible questions

3 Read the answers again and rate them.
- not so good.   ★☆☆☆☆
- good.   ★★★☆☆
- perfect – just what I needed to know. ★★★★★

PREPARE FOR TASK

4 a 💬 Work in pairs. Put the words in the correct order to make questions.

1 visit to best When town/city your is time the ?
2 the is make What way best new to friends ?
3 fast How I get really fit can ?

b 💬 Write answers to the questions. Compare your answers with the rest of the class. Who gave the best answer?

TASK

5 a 💬 Work in pairs. Write your own forum question. Share it with the class.

b Write an answer to the forum questions from the other pairs in the class.

6 Read all the answers to your question. Rate the answers using the star system in 3.

REPORT BACK

7 💬 Present and explain your ratings to the class.

→ Go to Review D, Unit 10, p. 136   **115**

11 A WORKING LIFE

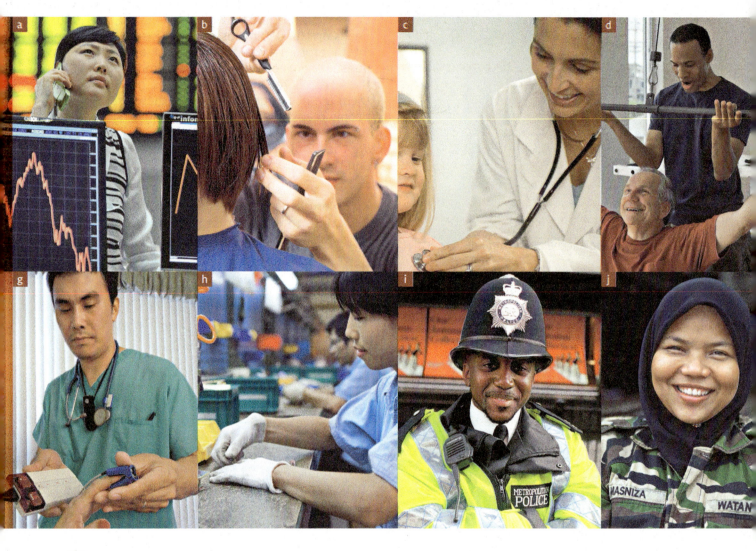

1. Work in pairs. Look at the photos. Do you think they are from
   1. an article about the current job situation?
   2. a website for a job agency?
   3. a poster selling university courses?

2. Work in pairs to complete A and B in the KEY VOCABULARY PANEL.

3. 11.1 Listen to Caleb, Bel and Krista talking about their jobs. Which job does each one do?

4. a Match the questions, 1–4, to answers a–d. Who gives each answer, Caleb, Bel or Krista?
   1. Where do you work?
   2. Do you like your job?
   3. What do you like about it?
   4. Why do you hate it?

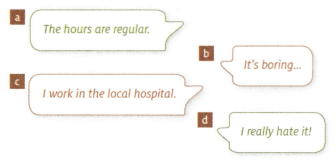

a The hours are regular.
b It's boring…
c I work in the local hospital.
d I really hate it!

b Listen again and check.

116

11.0

5 a Work in pairs. Ask and answer the quiz questions. What do you think the perfect job for your partner is?

What is your ideal job? Do our quick quiz and find out!
1 Do you prefer to work a) in a team? b) alone?
2 Are you happier working a) in an office? b) outside? c) from home?
3 Do you like a) giving orders? b) following orders?
4 Do you prefer to a) make things? b) sell things?
5 Do you like being a) active? b) creative? c) responsible for other people?
6 What's most important to you? a) money b) free time c) job satisfaction

b Report back to the class.

KEY VOCABULARY

Work & jobs

Occupations

A Match the photos to 12 of the jobs in the box.

hairdresser   chef   soldier   dentist   teacher
lawyer   banker   computer specialist   nurse
builder   factory worker   doctor   architect
police officer   waiter   company director
accountant   journalist   sports instructor
office worker

Discuss the questions. In which jobs do you
- work long hours?
- work regular hours?
- do hard physical work?
- work with money?
- travel a lot?
- make important decisions?
- help people?

NOTICE JOB & WORK

Job is countable. We say: *He has a great job!*
Work is uncountable. We say: *It's hard work.*
How do you say *job* and *work* in your language?

Adjectives to describe jobs

B Look at the adjectives to describe jobs. Match the adjectives to the jobs in A.

active   badly paid   boring   creative
dangerous   interesting   responsible
satisfying   stressful   well paid

Which job did you want to do as a child? Would you still like to do this job? Why/Why not?

117

11.1 THE HAPPIEST PROFESSION

- Practise superlative adjectives
- Compare different jobs

READING

1 💬 Work in pairs. Read the job satisfaction survey. Which three things do you think are the most important?

The job satisfaction survey
What's most important for you?
- ☐ friendly colleagues
- ☐ good pay
- ☐ a relaxed working atmosphere
- ☐ flexible hours
- ☐ a good boss
- ☐ being creative
- ☐ making a difference to people's lives
- ☐ good holidays

2 Look at the headline and the photo in the article below. Why do you think hairdressing is the happiest profession?

3 Read the article and check your answer in 2. Which three things in the survey in 1 are most important to hairdressers?

4 Mark the sentences true (T) or false (F).
1. Hairdressers don't work at the weekend.
2. Hairdressers are generally well paid.
3. Hairdressing is a creative job.
4. Being happy and friendly is part of the job.
5. Salons are often relaxed and friendly places.
6. Hairdressers usually wear formal clothes.

5 💬 Work in pairs. Discuss the questions.
- Is your hairdresser a happy person?
- Would you like to be a hairdresser? Why/Why not?

Hairdressing: the happiest profession

If you want to be happy in your job, be a hairdresser! A recent survey showed that hairdressing is the happiest profession in a list of over eighty different jobs.

But why? Is it the money? No. Hairdressing is certainly not one of the best-paid professions around. But hairdressers are a lot happier than doctors, lawyers or bankers, who are all better paid. So money isn't the answer. And it isn't the hours, either. Hairdressers often have to work long hours, and weekends are their busiest time.

So, what is the answer?

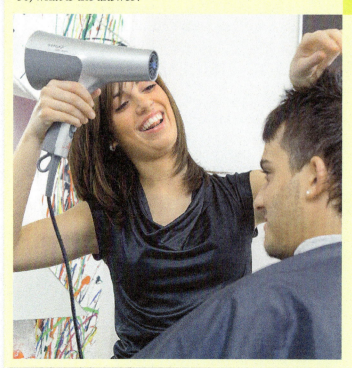

'I love my job because I make people happy quickly,' said one hairdresser. 'I love the creative side of the job – that's the most important thing for me,' said another. 'A good hairdresser chats with the customers, and smiles and jokes. It's a very important part of the job,' said the manager of one salon.

So it seems that a creative job with friendly workmates and a relaxed working atmosphere is much more important than the long hours and the low pay.

'I don't need to get up early in the morning, wear a suit and tie, or sit in front of a computer all day. The customers I work with are my best friends. When I'm in the salon, I feel like I'm at home! And you ask me why I'm happy?'

So, if you're unhappy in your job, or looking for a change of career, you know what to do! Become a hairdresser!

Grammar

1 a Mark the sentences true (T) or false (F).
1. Hairdressers and their customers are usually **best** friends.
2. A friendly smile is the **most important** thing for a good hairdresser.
3. Hairdressing is the **richest** profession.
4. Saturday is one of their **busiest** days.

b Complete 1–4 in the GRAMMAR PANEL with the words in **bold**.

2 a Work in pairs. Write the superlative form of the adjectives in brackets.
1. Who has the _____ (*creative*) job, an actor, a teacher or an architect?
2. Who has the _____ (*easy*) job, a nurse, a builder or a soldier?
3. Which do you think is the _____ (*interesting*) job, reporter, chef or film director?
4. Which is the _____ (*old*) job, doctor, lawyer, soldier or teacher?

b Ask and answer the questions.

3 Write two more similar questions. Ask and answer with the rest of the class.

SUPERLATIVE ADJECTIVES

We use superlative adjectives to compare or contrast something with all the other items in a group:

Hairdressers have the happiest profession. (= Hairdressers are happier than people with other professions.)

Forming superlative adjectives

One syllable: adjective + *-est*
old → oldest   rich → (1) _____

Two syllables ending in *-y*: change *-y* to *-i* and add *-est*
happy → happiest   busy → (2) _____

Two syllables or more: *most* + adjective
important → (3) _____

Irregular adjectives

good → (4) _____   bad → worst

We often use *the* or possessive adjectives (*my*, *your*, *his*) with superlative adjectives:
*It's **the** best job.*   *She's **my** best friend.*

See page 150 for grammar reference and more practice.

Speaking & Listening

1 Work in pairs. Look at the photo. This person is a member of the second happiest profession. Discuss the questions.
- What does she do?
- What is she doing in the photo?
- Why do you think she enjoys her job?

2 a Which do you think are the other top five happiest and unhappiest occupations?

b 11.2 Listen to the news report and compare your answers.

3 a Look at the jobs in the box. Which are
1. the five worst-paid jobs in the UK?
2. the five best-paid jobs?
3. the five most stressful jobs?

air traffic controllers   bankers   best-selling writers
call centre workers   celebrities   cleaners
fast-food restaurant staff   footballers   hairdressers
inner-city teachers   junior doctors   lawyers
miners   police officers   school cooks

b Turn to page 161 to check your answers. Were you surprised by any of the answers? Do you think the answers are different for your country?

11.1

119

11.2 DREAM JOB

- Practise *will/won't* for the future
- Discuss 'dream' jobs

LISTENING & SPEAKING

1 a Work in pairs. Look at the job advertisement. Discuss the questions.
- What does a caretaker usually do?
- What do you think an island caretaker does?
- Why do you think this is 'the best job ever'?

Vacancy
Island Caretaker
- six-month contract
- AUD$150,000
- live on a tropical island

The best job ever

b 11.3 Listen to two people discussing the job and check your answers.

2 a Listen again. Tick the things they talk about.

salary	☐	qualifications	☐
other benefits	☐	hours	☐
contract	☐	responsibilities	☐
training	☐		

b Compare your answers with a partner. Can you remember what the people said about each item?

3 Do you agree that this is 'the best job ever'? Why/Why not?

It looks beautiful, but I think living on an island is very boring... or very lonely!

GRAMMAR

1 Complete the sentences with the correct option.

The winning candidate
1 will / won't need to pay for a place to live.
2 will / won't earn a good salary.
3 will / won't work a lot of hours.
4 will / won't use the internet.
5 will / won't have a long contract.

2 Read transcript 11.3 on pages 166–167. Underline examples of *will*, *won't* and *'ll*. Complete 1–7 in the GRAMMAR PANEL.

3 a Complete the job description with *will* or *won't*.

Position Vacant
Professional ice cream taster

☐ **The ideal candidate**
(1) _____ need any formal qualifications.
(2) _____ have experience in the job.
(3) _____ have any food allergies.

☐ **As part of the job he or she**
(4) _____ taste over 100 ice creams a day.
(5) _____ help create new flavours.
(6) _____ discuss recipes or ingredients with anyone outside the company.

b Work in pairs. Compare your answers. Which do you think is the best job, the island caretaker or the ice cream taster? Why?

4 a Work in pairs. Think of another 'dream job'. Write a short job description. Include the information in the box.

job title   location   salary   abilities
qualifications   duties and responsibilities

b Compare your job with the rest of the class. Which do you think is the best job? Why?

WILL/WON'T

We use *will/won't* + infinitive to talk about what we know and think about the future:
The winning candidate will receive a salary of $150,000.
It'll be a fun job.

The contracted form of *will* + *not* is (1) _____ :
Glenn won't get the job. He can't swim.

The contraction of *will* is (2) _____ .

We use *'ll* after names and pronouns:
Tom will win. → *Tom* (3) _____ *win.*
He will enjoy the job. → *He* (4) _____ *enjoy the job.*

+	You (5) _____ receive a good salary.
−	He (6) _____ receive a good salary.
?	(7) _____ he receive a good salary?

See page 150 for grammar reference and more practice.

11.2

PRONUNCIATION: *will, 'll, won't*

1 🔊 11.4 Listen to a short interview with a professional whale-watcher. Would you like to do his job? Why/Why not?

2 a Complete the dialogue with *will*, *'ll* or *won't*.

A So, tell me about your new job.
B Well, I _____ start until next year. First I _____ fly to Oslo to do a three-week training course, and then I _____ travel to the north, where I _____ be on my own for four months.
A You mean you _____ see anybody for four months!
B No, I _____ . But I _____ have a satellite connection to talk to my family and my colleagues at base camp.
A _____ your family go over to Norway, too?
B Yes, they _____ . For a short visit in the spring.

b Listen again and check.

3 a Work in pairs. Notice when the full form of *will* is used. Match the examples to the rules.

We use the full form of *will*
1 in questions   a *But I will have a satellite connection.*
2 in short answers   b *Will your family go over, too?*
3 for emphasis   c *Yes, they will.*

b 🔊 11.5 Listen and repeat.

4 💬 Work in pairs. Practise repeating the interview.

SPEAKING

1 💬 Work in pairs. Look at the photos and answer the questions.
- What are the jobs?
- Do you agree that they are all 'dream jobs'?
- Which do you think is the hardest job? Why?
- What, in your opinion, is the best job in the world? Why?

121

11.3 THE CHANGING WORKPLACE

- PRACTISE WILL/WON'T & MIGHT/MIGHT NOT FOR PREDICTIONS
- DISCUSS WORK CONDITIONS IN THE FUTURE

SPEAKING & VOCABULARY: Work conditions

1 Answer the questions. Use a dictionary to help you.

Do you know anyone who
- works a four-day week?
- works from home?
- works for himself/herself?
- runs a business?
- has a part-time job?
- has a temporary contract?
- has a permanent position?
- is unemployed?

2 Work in pairs. Ask and answer the questions in 1. Use the questions in the box to find out more information.

> Where does he/she work?
> What does he/she do?
> Who does he/she work for?
> Does he/she like his/her job?
> Would he/she like to change jobs?
> What kind of job is he/she looking for?

READING

1 Work in pairs. Read the first paragraph of the article. Which three predictions do you think will be in the article?

2 Read predictions 1–10. Are any of them the same as your suggestions in 1?

3 Read the predictions again. Which do you think
- are already true?
- will soon be true?
- will possibly be true at some time in the future?

Top Ten Predictions: The World of Work

We live in a world where everything changes very quickly. The world of work is no exception. We asked ten experts to give us their predictions about the biggest changes we can expect in the world of work over the next ten years.

1. All office workers will work a four-day week.
2. Working conditions and salaries will get worse.
3. More and more people will work from home.
4. Companies will only offer part-time and temporary contracts.
5. People won't retire until they are 75 or 80 years old.
6. Computer skills will be essential for all jobs.
7. Candidates for top jobs will need to speak at least two or three languages.
8. Many young people will need to travel to another country to find a job.
9. A university education won't guarantee a good job.
10. Finding a stable, permanent position won't be easy.

What do you think?

Post your comments below (56 comments)

11.3

4 Read the comments. Which prediction(s) are they referring to? Do you agree with the comments? Why/Why not?

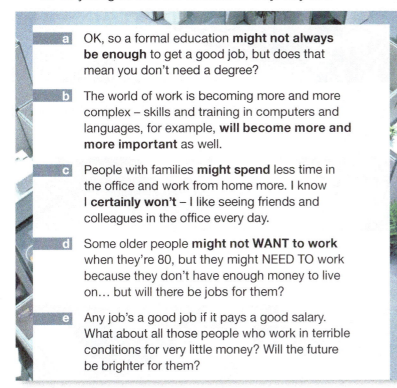

a OK, so a formal education **might not always be enough** to get a good job, but does that mean you don't need a degree?

b The world of work is becoming more and more complex – skills and training in computers and languages, for example, **will become more and more important** as well.

c People with families **might spend** less time in the office and work from home more. I know **I certainly won't** – I like seeing friends and colleagues in the office every day.

d Some older people **might not WANT to work** when they're 80, but they might NEED TO work because they don't have enough money to live on… but will there be jobs for them?

e Any job's a good job if it pays a good salary. What about all those people who work in terrible conditions for very little money? Will the future be brighter for them?

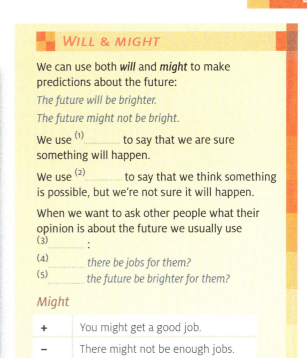

WILL & MIGHT

We can use both *will* and *might* to make predictions about the future:
The future will be brighter.
The future might not be bright.

We use (1) .... to say that we are sure something will happen.

We use (2) .... to say that we think something is possible, but we're not sure it will happen.

When we want to ask other people what their opinion is about the future we usually use (3) .... :

(4) .... *there be jobs for them?*
(5) .... *the future be brighter for them?*

Might

+	You might get a good job.
–	There might not be enough jobs.

See page 150 for grammar reference and more practice.

GRAMMAR

1 Work in pairs. Look at the phrases in bold in the comments above. Do the writers think
  1 this will definitely happen?
  2 it's possible, but they're not sure?

> **NOTICE** DEFINITELY + WILL/WON'T
> We often use *definitely* with *will/won't* to stress that we are certain of what we're saying:
> *I'll definitely study English again next year.*
> *I definitely won't stay up late tonight.*

2 Underline the other examples of *will* and *might*. Complete 1–5 in the GRAMMAR PANEL.

3 Complete the predictions using *will/won't* or *might/might not*.
  1 It .... rain tomorrow.
  2 I .... go to bed early tonight.
  3 I .... have a lot of work to do tomorrow.
  4 I .... do some English homework this evening.
  5 I .... have a (new) job next year.

4 a Work in small groups. Write three more predictions about the future of work. Use *will* or *might*.

  b Share your predictions with the class. Which predictions do you think
  1 will definitely come true?
  2 might never come true?

SPEAKING

1 Work in pairs. Look at the photo. What is the woman doing? What do you think she can see?

2 Work in pairs. Discuss the questions.
  • Is fortune-telling popular in your country?
  • If yes, what kind of fortune-telling (cards, horoscopes) and where (on TV, in newspapers and magazines, on the streets)?
  • Do people take it seriously or is it just for fun? If not, why not?

3 a Work in pairs.
  Student A: you are a fortune-teller. Tell your partner's fortune. Turn to page 161.
  Student B: prepare questions to ask the fortune-teller. Turn to page 159.

  b Exchange roles.

4 Tell the class what the fortune-teller predicted for you. Were you happy with the predictions? Why/Why not?

123

11.4 FUNCTIONAL LANGUAGE: OFFERS AND REQUESTS

TUNE IN

1 **a** Work in pairs. Match the verbs to the objects. Use a dictionary to help you.

  1 load/unload   a the dishes
  2 set/clear   b the dishwasher
  3 take out   c the table
  4 wash/dry   d the rubbish/recycling

  b Look at the pictures. Which household task does each image show?

2 **a** 💬 Which of the tasks do you have to do
  1 every day?
  2 every two or three days?
  3 never – somebody else does it for me!

  b Ask and answer with a partner. What other tasks do you do in the house? Who does more housework, you or your partner?

  How often do you have to wash the dishes?
  Never. We have a dishwasher!

3 🔊 11.6 Listen to four short conversations. What household tasks are the people talking about?

4 Listen again. Match the conversations to the people who are talking.
  a a mother and son
  b a married couple
  c a father and daughter
  d a host and guest

FOCUS ON LANGUAGE

5 **a** Read the sentences. Are they requests (R) or offers (O)?
  1 **Will you** clear the table first, please?
  2 **Let me** wash the dishes.
  3 **I'll** load the dishwasher then.
  4 **Can you** come and set the table?

  b Look at the phrases in **bold**. Which are
  a asking someone to do something?
  b offering to do something?

6 Put the words in the correct order to make requests or offers.
  1 you with help Let that me bag
  2 me do Will you a favour ?
  3 please the door open Can for me you ?
  4 you that I'll for do

> ### Asking & offering
> 🔊 11.7 Listen to the requests and offers in **6**. <u>Underline</u> the main stress.
> *Let me <u>help</u> you with that <u>bag</u>.*
> Listen again and repeat.
> Notice that the verb in all these sentences is in the **infinitive**.

7 Work in pairs. Write a request or an offer for each of the situations. Use the language in **5** and **6**.
  1 You see someone carrying a lot of heavy books.
  2 You want to leave the room. Your hands are full. The door is closed.
  3 Your friend is having problems with an exercise.
  4 You need some help with your computer.
  5 Your friend is going to get a coffee from the coffee machine. You'd like one, too.

OVER TO YOU

8 💬 Work in pairs. Act out the situations in **7**. Respond to the requests or offers.

9 💬 When was the last time you offered someone help? What help did he/she need?

124

Speaking task: an action plan   11.5

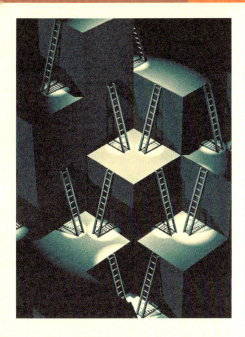

Tune in

1 Look at the image. What can you see? What do you think is the connection between the image and the world of work?

2 Read the article and check your answers in 1.

3 Read the article again. Is it
   1 giving useful information?
   2 asking important questions?
   3 advertising a training agency?

Upskilling for a new world of work

We live in a changing world. Jobs are changing, and the skills and qualifications you need to do the jobs are changing, too.

Notice
upskill = to learn or teach new skills. The word *up* gives the idea of progress and success:
Upskilling helps you get a better job and a better chance in life.

Using a computer, driving a car, having a school or university education, all these basic skills and qualifications are still important, but they're not enough.

There are so many new jobs and so many new ways of working. There are so many new markets and so many new products. You need to make sure you're learning the right skills for this new and changing world. You need to **upskill**.

Upskilling is equally important for people with or without a job. If you have a job, new skills will help you keep your job; if you don't have a job, **upskilling** will help you find one.

The most important thing is to know what these skills are – and how to get them. We can help you. We can tell you what you need to do and how best to do it. We can make sure your skills are the ones you need in tomorrow's world of work.

Click here now and open up a new world of work.

Upskilling: training for a new world.

Prepare for task

4 a Work in groups. Read the skills and qualifications in the box and answer the questions.
   • Which skills and qualifications can someone teach you?
   • Which can you teach yourself?
   • Which come naturally or with time?

   speaking one or more foreign languages
   computer skills   familiarity with the internet
   familiarity with other cultures and countries
   knowledge of a specialist technical area
   a university degree   a vocational qualification
   experience in your field   flexibility
   creativity   people skills

b Which three skills or qualifications do you think are the most important in today's job market? Why?

Task

5 Work in pairs. Discuss the questions.
   • Which of the skills or qualifications will be important for you in a possible future job? Why?
   • Which of these skills and qualifications do you already have? Which would you like to get?
   • What's the best and quickest way to get these skills and qualifications? How long do you think it will take?

6 Write a personal action plan for upskilling over the next two years. Decide which skills you want to focus on and how you plan to develop them. Write short notes.
   - *improve computer skills*
   - *look for evening/weekend course*

Report back

7 Present your action plans to the class. Whose plan sounds
   1 the most realistic?
   2 the most ambitious?

→ Go to Review D, Unit 11, p. 137   → Go to Writing bank 6, p. 157   125

12 Listmania!

1. 💬 Work in pairs. Look at the photos showing people's dreams and ambitions. Can you guess what they are? Check your answers in A in the KEY VOCABULARY PANEL.

2. 💬 Work in pairs. Answer the questions.
   1. How many of the ambitions would you like to do/have you done?
   2. Can you think of any other ambitions to add to the list?

3. Complete this sentence so that it is true for you.
   My greatest ambition is to…

4. 💬 Find out what your classmates' dreams and ambitions are. Which is the most common ambition? Which is the strangest?

5. Work in pairs to complete B in the KEY VOCABULARY PANEL.

126

12.0

KEY VOCABULARY

Dreams & ambitions

A Match the photos to six of the ambitions below.

Top ten lifetime ambitions

1. do a parachute jump
2. write a best-seller
3. run a marathon
4. have a big family
5. build your own dream home
6. go on a round-the-world trip
7. be your own boss
8. make a fortune
9. direct a film
10. speak at least three languages

NOTICE *own*

We often use *own* with a possessive adjective:
*I want to be **my own** boss.*
Don't use *own* with *a* or *the*: *He built a/the own dream home.*
How do you say *own* in your language?

REVIEW: Common verbs & collocations

B Complete the lists of nouns in the circles. Some nouns go in more than one circle. Use a dictionary to help you.

~~dinner~~   a shower   a living   an exercise   lunch   the bus
a list   a message   a phone call   a rest   a (great) job
notes   the housework   a holiday   some work   children
a good time   a taxi   the shopping   a mistake
some cooking   money

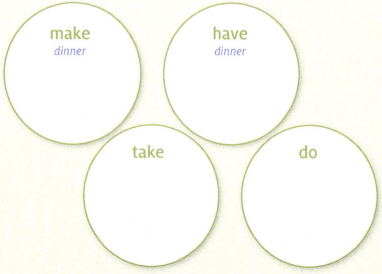

- Which of these common collocations would be different in your language?

In Spanish, we don't say 'have dinner' or 'have lunch', we have a special verb for those.

6 🔊 **12.1** Listen to Mared talking about what she did yesterday.

1. Which of the common collocations does she use?
2. Which of the ambitions on the list has she achieved?

7 💬 Work in pairs. Tell each other what you did yesterday. Use as many of the collocations as you can.

127

12.1 ONE HUNDRED AND ONE...

- PRACTISE THE PRESENT PERFECT
- TALK ABOUT ACHIEVEMENTS & AMBITIONS

SPEAKING

1 Work in small groups. Discuss the questions.
- When did you last write a list?
- What kind of list was it (a shopping list, a list of things to do, a list of presents to buy, etc.)?
- What was on the list?

2 12.2 Listen to someone answering the questions in 1. What kind of list is the person talking about?

READING & SPEAKING

1 Look at the book covers. Match them to the book review extracts.
1 'This is *the* ultimate shopping list!'
2 'More of a travel guide than a list – but then, everything's a list these days!'
3 'The only problem is, will there ever be time to listen to them all?'
4 'No surprises on this short list, but lots of good examples for living a long and happy life.'

2 In which of the books do these items appear?
1 the Great Wall of China
2 give more than you take
3 the first Radiohead LP
4 the finest diamond ring

3 Think of three more items for the lists in each book. Which book (if any) would you like to read? Why?

4 Read another list. What do you think is the missing verb?

5 a Read the list again. Which of the activities
  a include animals?
  b can only happen in a specific place?
  c include a long journey?
  d include a form of transport?
  e can be dangerous?

  b Which of the items on the list
  - would you like to do?
  - would you not like to do? Why not?

6 Rewrite the list with your personal top ten. Compare your list with the class.

Top Ten Things to ___ Before You Die
1 Go whale-watching
2 Ride a camel to the pyramids
3 Fly over a volcano
4 Drive a Formula One car
5 See the Northern Lights
6 Go skydiving
7 Explore Antarctica
8 Take the Trans-Siberian railway
9 Swim with dolphins
10 Ride a horse along a beach

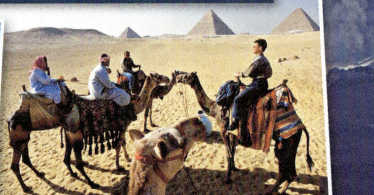

Listening

1 a 🔊 12.3 Listen to three people, Hanna, Renata and Stephen, talking about the list in READING & SPEAKING 4. Which activities do they talk about?

b 💬 Work in pairs. Compare your answers. Do you think Hanna, Renata and Stephen like the list? Why/Why not?

2 a Listen again. Complete the extracts.

HANNA	I _____ these lists.
RENATA	I think they're _____ .
HANNA	Life isn't a _____ .
STEPHEN	Some people think that life is just about _____ .
HANNA	I'd love to go _____ .
STEPHEN	I'd love to see _____ .

b 💬 Do you agree with what they say?

Grammar

1 Mark the sentences Hanna (H), Renata (R) or Stephen (S).
1 **Has he ever been** to Antarctica? Yes, **he has**.
2 They **haven't been** whale-watching, but they'd love to go.
3 **Have you ever seen** the Northern Lights? No, **I haven't**, but **I've seen** the midnight sun.
4 She**'s visited** Finland.
5 They**'ve travelled** a lot.

2 Work in pairs. Look at the words in **bold** in 1. Complete 1–10 in the GRAMMAR PANEL.

3 a <u>Underline</u> the past participles in the questions.

Have you ever...
1 written a novel, a poem or a song?
2 worked in a bar?
3 won a prize?
4 travelled to another continent?
5 flown in a helicopter?
6 spoken in public?
7 lived in another country?
8 taught something to someone?
9 run a marathon?

b Which past participles are regular and which are irregular? What is the infinitive of the irregular past participles?

4 💬 Work in pairs. Ask and answer the questions in 3a.

PRESENT PERFECT: HAVE YOU EVER...?

We use the present perfect to talk about past experiences:
Have you ever been to Antarctica?
No, **I haven't**, but **I've been** to Argentina.

We form the present perfect with **have/has** + past participle.

+	I/You/We/They (1)_____ been to Antarctica. He/She/It **'s** been to Antarctica.
–	I/You/We/They (2)_____ seen whales. He/She/It **hasn't** seen whales.
?	(3)_____ you ever been to Argentina? (4)_____ she ever been to Argentina?
Yes/No	Yes, I have./No, I (5)_____ . Yes, she (6)_____ ./No, she **hasn't**.

Past participles

We form the past participle of regular verbs by adding **-ed** to the infinitive of the verb:
travel → (7)_____ , visit → (8)_____

Some verbs are irregular:
see → (9)_____ , go → gone/ (10)_____

See page 151 for grammar reference and more practice.

Speaking

1 a Work in pairs. Write a new list on one of the topics.

Top five most...
- exciting things I've seen
- difficult sports I've played
- terrible places I've visited
- boring things I've done
- interesting people I've met

b Write questions for the five points on your list using *Have you ever...?*

I've been to a World Cup final.
Have you ever seen an important football match live?

2 💬 Ask and answer questions with the rest of the class. Has anybody else done all the things on your list?

129

12.2 THE BEST CITY?

■ PRACTISE THE PRESENT PERFECT & PAST SIMPLE
■ DESCRIBE CITIES & TALK ABOUT LIFE EXPERIENCES

READING & VOCABULARY: Describing places

1 a Read the phrases in the box. Which would you normally use to describe
1 the city?   2 the country?   3 either the city or the country?

Use a dictionary to help you.

> relaxed atmosphere   state-of-the-art airport   beautiful trees   cosmopolitan culture
> top-quality hotels   fresh air   wonderful lakes

b Which phrases can you use to describe where you live?

2 Work in pairs. Look at the photos of two different cities. Discuss the questions.
1 What can you see in the two photos?
2 What do the cities have in common?
3 Which of the phrases in 1 can you use in your descriptions?
4 Do you know where these cities might be?

City 1

City 2

3 A style magazine recently voted these the top two cities in the world to live in. Read the texts. Complete the sentences with the correct option.

City 1

Zurich is our number one choice. It has a transport system that is the best in the world. And because this is Switzerland, the trains are always on time! Now the city is expanding its tram system and state-of-the-art airport. It is also a world leader in protecting the climate. There is fresh air here, wonderful lakes and green hills all around.

City 2

Last year's winner is now number two, but Copenhagen is a city we still love. There is interesting architecture, very little crime and a relaxed atmosphere in a perfect location. It's great to bike your way around the city's cycle paths. The city is clean and green, and a fantastic place to live in. Like so many cities in Scandinavia, it has a very cosmopolitan culture.

1 The most important thing for the magazine when it chose these cities was
   a cultural life.   b the environment.   c tourist attractions.
2 Other aspects the magazine thinks are important include
   a transport.   b climate.   c the cost of living.
3 The two cities are similar because
   a they are modern and sophisticated.   b they have a great natural setting.   c they have many business possibilities.

4 a What things are important when choosing a town/city to live in? Put the items in the box in order of importance to make your 'top ten'.

> job opportunities   location   climate   cultural life   safety   size   shopping   environment
> people   food   transport service/connections   atmosphere   schools and universities

b Work in pairs. Compare your lists. If you disagree with each other, defend your choice.

The most important thing is job opportunities. A beautiful, green, clean city is great – if you have a job.

5 Think about your home town/city. Is it a possible candidate for one of the top ten towns/cities? Why/Why not?

12.2

LISTENING

1 🔊 **12.4** Listen to two travel writers, Gus and Maria, talking about the two cities.

1 Which city are they each talking about?
2 Are they generally positive or negative?
3 Which person has visited the city already?

2 Listen again and answer the questions.

1 What does Gus like about the city?
2 What does he like about the people?
3 When did Maria go to Zurich?
4 What doesn't she like about the city?
5 What type of city does she prefer?

3 💬 Work in pairs. Make a list of the top five cities you would like to visit. Compare your lists. Are your tastes the same?

My number one city is Rio. I've always wanted to see Copacabana beach.

NOTICE ALWAYS + PRESENT PERFECT

We can use *always* with the present perfect:
I've always wanted to visit Rome.
I've always loved Italy.

GRAMMAR

1 a Work in pairs. Read the extracts and answer the questions.

> I **went** to Zurich a few years ago, but I didn't like it much. I didn't have a very good time there.

> I**'ve been** to other cities in Europe which I like more… Berlin, for example.

1 Do we know when Maria went to Zurich?
2 Do we know when she went to Berlin?

b Choose the correct option to complete 1–5 in the GRAMMAR PANEL .

2 a Read the present perfect questions. Match them to the past simple follow-up questions.

1 Have you ever won a prize?
2 Have you ever given a presentation?
3 Have you ever met a famous person?
4 Have you ever been in an accident?
5 Have you ever worked in an office?
6 Have you ever run a long-distance race?

a Did you enjoy it?
b What happened exactly?
c What did you do there?
d What was it about?
e Who was it?
f What did you win?

b 💬 Work in pairs. Ask and answer the questions. Ask two more follow-up questions.

PRONUNCIATION: Present perfect & past simple

1 a 🔊 **12.5** Listen to six statements. <u>Underline</u> the verb you hear.

1 lived / 've lived
2 worked / 've worked
3 studied / 's studied
4 had / 've had
5 read / 's read
6 visited / 've visited

b Listen again and repeat.

PRESENT PERFECT & PAST SIMPLE

We use the (1)*present perfect / past simple* to talk about our past experiences:
I've been to other cities in Europe.

We (2)*give / don't give* a specific time in the past:
I've been to Rome last year.

We use the (3)*present perfect / past simple* if we say when something happened:
I went to Zurich a few years ago.

We use the (4)*present perfect / past simple* to ask an initial question about past experiences:
Have you ever been to Thailand?
Yes, I have.

We use the (5)*present perfect / past simple* to ask for more information:
Did you have a good time there?
It was OK.

See page 151 for grammar reference and more practice.

12.3 WHAT A FEAT!

- REVIEW VERB FORMS
- TALK ABOUT ACTIVITIES & ABILITIES

SPEAKING & LISTENING

1 a Look at the photos from a video clip of a sporting event. Answer the questions.
   1 What kind of event do you think it is?
   2 Which country do you think holds the most famous event?

b 12.6 Listen to the video clip commentary. Check your answers.

2 a Listen again and complete the statements.
   1 There are .... sports in a triathlon.
   2 The first .... - .... triathlon took place in Hawaii in 19.......... .
   3 Finally the contestants have to run .... km.
   4 Women .... take part in the Ironman World Championship.

b Why do you think people take part in the Ironman World Championship? Would you like to?

3 Read a blog entry about Klaus Sanderling who is preparing for the Ironman World Championship. Why does he think he's lucky?

4 a List five things you think Klaus needs to do before taking part in the triathlon.

b 12.7 Listen to an interview with Klaus talking about his preparations for the Ironman World Championship and check your answers.

HAWAII, HERE I GO!
Klaus Sanderling
13 February
Big news today! I'm the luckiest man alive! Today I found out that I will be in the starting line-up at Kailua-Kona in Hawaii in October. Yippee! Just 1,800 people have the chance to do this and thousands apply. Now the only problem is starting training!

5 Listen again and correct the statements.
   1 To enter the lottery, you need to do a full Ironman race somewhere in the world.
   2 He began as a cyclist.
   3 Running is his worst sport.
   4 On Fridays he usually rests.
   5 On Sundays he runs about 10 km.
   6 The weather will be cold when he does the triathlon.

12.3

Grammar

1 Complete the sentences with the correct form of the verb in brackets.
1. I .... (start) with normal triathlons, like a lot of people, and I realised that I .... (be) quite good.
2. For the next six months I .... (follow) a very strict programme.
3. On Wednesdays I usually .... (go) for a short run, around 10 to 12 km.
4. Then, on Sundays I .... (run) a longer distance, about 20 km.
5. You .... (can) wear swimsuits made from certain material because they give you an advantage.
6. Right now I .... (run) with lots of clothes on to prepare myself for the heat.
7. In Hawaii the weather .... (be) hot.

2 a Check your answers in transcript 12.7 on page 167. Match the verbs in 1 to the verb forms, a–f, in the GRAMMAR PANEL .

b Match verb forms a–f to functions 1–6 in the GRAMMAR PANEL .

3 Read what Eli has to say about being a DJ. Why does she enjoy it?

I began deejaying when I was 14. I usually deejay twice a week. I didn't have a teacher, I taught myself. I've always loved dance music, that's how I started. When you're working, you can do what you like, there aren't any rules, but you can't take your eyes off the dance floor. You have to see what music the people like and what they're dancing to. Right now, I'm deejaying in two clubs. It's just a hobby for me, but I'm going to try and deejay in the future in different towns and cities. Whatever happens, I know I will always be a DJ.

4 a Read the text again. <u>Underline</u> the verb forms in the text and complete the questions.
1. When .... (begin)?
2. Why .... (start) it?
3. How often .... (do) it?
4. Who .... (be) your teacher or guide?
5. .... (be) there any rules to follow?
6. Where .... (do) it right now?
7. What .... you .... (try) and do in the future?
8. .... (be) a DJ in five years' time?

b Work in pairs. Check your answers. Take it in turns to role-play an interview with Eli.

Review of verbs

We use the following verb forms
a the present simple
b the present continuous
c the past simple
d *going to*
e *will*
f *can*

to talk about
1 ability and permission.
2 what happened at a specific time in the past.
3 what we are doing now.
4 future plans.
5 what we know or think about the future.
6 things we do regularly.

See page 151 for grammar reference and more practice.

Speaking

1 Think of an activity you can do well – a sport, a job, an interest, a hobby or something you're studying. Answer the questions in GRAMMAR 4a.

2 a Work in pairs. Ask and answer the questions. Write down the answers. Use the prompts to help you.
- X began… when…
- X started… because…
- X usually…
- X's teacher…
- X says you can/can't…
- Now X… every week/month.
- X's going to… in the future.
- X will always…

b Tell the rest of the class the information you find out about your partner.

3 What kind of abilities do your classmates have? Are they similar or different to yours?

133

12.4 FUNCTIONAL LANGUAGE: FINDING OUT AND RECOMMENDING

Tune in

1 💬 You want to go away for the weekend to a city you haven't been to before. How do you get information about where to go? Look at the photos for ideas.

2 Match the photos to the ideas.
1 look up the city online
2 take a friend's advice
3 read a guidebook about the city
4 read the travel section of the newspaper
5 go to a travel agent's

3 🔊 12.8 Listen to Roisin asking some friends, Monica, Petra and Lily, about where to go.
1 Which city or cities does each friend recommend?
2 What reasons does each give for her choice?
3 What city does Roisin decide on in the end?

4 Listen again and correct the statements.
1 Monica's been to Antwerp.
2 Antwerp is similar to Amsterdam now.
3 Roisin and Mark went to Paris five years ago.
4 Roisin's been to Copenhagen a few times.
5 Lily's never lived in Bologna.
6 The weather's good there all year round.

> **"Let me see/Let me think"**
>
> 🔊 12.9 Listen to the extract from one of the conversations.
> *I wanted something a bit different.*
> *Oh, I see. Let me think... Copenhagen?*
>
> Does the speaker's voice go up ↗ or down ↘?
> Which word do we stress? Where are the pauses?
>
> How do you say *let me see/let me think* in your language?

Focus on language

5 a Match the responses, a–c, to Roisin's questions, 1–3.
1 Where do you recommend?
2 Have you been there?
3 I've never been there. What's it like?

a Yes, of course! I lived there, don't you remember?
b Beautiful nature, the people are great... a fantastic place!
c Well, I've never been, but everyone says Antwerp's great.

b 🔊 12.10 Listen and check.

> **NOTICE** WHAT'S IT LIKE?
> We use *What's it like?* to ask for a description of something.
> We can use the same question about people, too:
> *What's she/he like?*
> How do you say *What's it/she/he like?* in your language?

Over to you

6 💬 Work in pairs. Ask for information about a place to go for the weekend.
Student A: ask the questions in 5a.
Student B: recommend a place that you know.

7 💬 Take turns to recommend something else to your partner – a restaurant, a book, a film, a website, etc.

WRITING TASK: LANGUAGE LEARNING TIPS 12.5

Top five tips for learning a language

1. First of all, make sure you always arrive for class on time.
2. Remember to do all your homework, especially the grammar exercises. Ask for extra homework if there's something you need more practice in. Remember, practice makes perfect!
3. Keep a vocabulary notebook. Write down any new words you learn in class. Carry it around with you. Study it when you're on the bus or in a queue at the bank, or when you're having a coffee at work.
4. Make sure you understand everything in class. Make notes and study them as soon as you get home.
5. Last, but not least, keep a diary. Write about what you did in class, what you learned and what you had problems with. At the end of the course, you'll be surprised to see how much you've learned!

TUNE IN

1. Look at the photos. What do they say about learning a language? What is more important for you, studying the grammar or speaking the language? Why?

2. a Read the tips for making the most of your language lessons. Which person, a or b, do you think wrote them?

   b Work in pairs. Compare your answers. Do you think they are good tips? Why/Why not?

3. Work in pairs. The person who wrote the tips in 2a is looking for a new language course. Which of the items do you think is more important for him/her?
   - technology in the classroom
   - a good atmosphere in class
   - a good coursebook, with clear grammar and practical everyday English
   - interesting topics to talk about
   - plenty of opportunities to speak

4. Read the list in 3 again. Which of these things do you think helped you most on this course? Why? What else helped you to learn?

PREPARE FOR TASK

5. a Work in small groups. Write a list of things you can do when you finish your course to help you keep improving your English.
   Watch films in English, organise a language exchange, do an online course...

   b Which are the five most motivating ways to study outside the classroom?

6. a Read the tips in 2a again and find
   1. the phrase used to introduce the first point.
   2. the phrase used to introduce the last point.
   3. a well-known saying about learning.
   4. at least five imperative verbs.

   b What do you notice about the style of writing?

TASK

7. Work in the same groups as in 5. Write a tip sheet called 'Five things to improve your English outside class'. Use your notes in 5 and the language in 6a.

REPORT BACK

8. a Share your tip sheet with the class. Answer the questions in your group.
   1. Do other groups have similar tips?
   2. Which new tip or tips do you like best? Why?
   3. Which tips do you think you will follow when you finish the course?

   b Share your ideas with the class.

→ Go to Review D, Unit 12, p. 138   135

Review D Unit 10

Vocabulary
Technology

1 💬 Work in pairs. Think of ten gadgets. Answer the questions.
Which
1 can't you live without?
2 do you really hate?
Why?

Communication

2 Look at the groups of verbs. Which verb in each group is not part of that lexical set? Why is it different?
1 call   answer   phone   ring
2 email   write   call   text
3 respond   answer   phone   reply

3 a Choose a verb in 2 to complete the sentences.
1 I usually .... because it's quicker than calling and it's cheaper.
2 Sometimes people don't .... my emails and I think it's because they don't get them.
3 Nobody .... anymore and that's a shame. I love receiving letters.
4 I hate the telephone. If it .... all the time it can make me very nervous.

b 💬 Are these sentences true for you? Discuss your answers with a partner.

Adjectives

4 a Read the advice. Complete the sentences with a suitable adjective.
1 It's better to buy a s............ computer, like a laptop. It's more convenient than a desktop.
2 You don't need to buy an e............ computer. There are cheap ones that are equally good.
3 The most important thing about a laptop is the weight. It's best to get a l............ one.

b 💬 Do you think this is good advice? Think of more advice about buying computers.

5 Write three sentences of advice to someone who wants to buy one of the items in the box.

a car   a bike   a music player   a TV

Grammar
Comparative adjectives

1 a Work in pairs. Write sentences comparing the pairs of things.
1 two rival football teams
2 two nearby towns/cities
3 two gadgets

b 💬 Compare your sentences with other students.

2 Think of technology now and in the past. Write a short paragraph on the role that technology plays in your life.
Before I didn't have a computer, now I can't live without one. It's easier to keep in touch with everybody now through email and cheaper to call as well...

Going to

3 a Look at the activities in the box. Tick the ones that you are going to do today or tomorrow.

read the newspaper   have a coffee   get a bus
listen to the radio   have a shower   call a friend
go shopping   go to work   go to class

b 💬 Compare your answers with a partner. What else are you going to do?

Functional language
Giving instructions

1 🔊 R15 Look at the photo. Listen to some instructions. What is the gadget and how does it work?

2 💬 Practise explaining the gadget to a partner.

▪ Looking back

- What did you discover in this unit about technology?
- Think of six different forms of communication and six different situations in which they would be appropriate.
- Think of three things you can say about your plans for the next few days.

UNIT 11

REVIEW D

VOCABULARY
Work & jobs

1 Work in pairs. Think of a job that matches all three adjectives.

 1 well paid stressful interesting
 2 satisfying creative badly paid
 3 physical responsible dangerous

2 💬 Think of five close friends or family members who work. Write down the names of the jobs they do. Explain the list to a partner.

Doctor – my uncle's a doctor. He works at the hospital. He loves his job.

3 a Work in pairs. Match the expressions to their opposites.

 1 work in an office   a work part-time
 2 work long hours   b work alone
 3 work in a team   c do a desk job
 4 do hard physical work   d follow orders
 5 make important decisions   e work outside

b 💬 Think of jobs where you have to do each of the things in the two lists. Which job(s) would you never do? Why?

Work conditions

4 💬 Work in two groups. Look at the work situations below.

Group A: discuss the advantages of each one.
Group B: discuss the disadvantages of each one.

• a four-day week
• a part-time job
• running your own business
• working from home

5 a 💬 Work in pairs with one student from group A and one student from group B. Compare your ideas.

b Discuss the questions.
• Which of the four situations would you prefer to work in?
• Why?

GRAMMAR
Superlative adjectives

1 Make sentences to compare the jobs in the photos. Use the correct form of the words in the box.

good   boring   easy   exciting   stressful   bad   difficult   well paid

I think the DJ has the best job!
I think the air steward has the most boring job.

Will & might

2 a Complete the sentences using *will/won't*.

> On my next birthday, I _____ be (add your age) _____ . I _____ have a big party. I _____ get a lot of presents. I _____ take a few days' holiday. I'm sure I _____ have a great time.

b When can you replace *will/won't* with *might/might not*? Which is the best answer for you? Compare your answers with a partner.

FUNCTIONAL LANGUAGE
Offers & requests

1 a Work in pairs. Complete the requests and offers using one word.

 1 _____ me help you with that. It looks really heavy.
 2 _____ you give me another one of those? They're really delicious.
 3 _____ you hold this for me, please? My hands are full.
 4 Don't worry. I _____ get some when I go out.
 5 Will you do me a favour, _____ ? Can you get the keys from my pocket? Thanks.

b 🔊 R16 💬 Listen and check. What exactly do you think is happening in situations 1–5 in 1a? What do you think the other person says in response? Act out the situations with a partner.

◆ LOOKING BACK

• What's the most useful thing you've learned in this unit? Why is it useful?
• Which exercise was a) the most interesting? b) the easiest? Why?
• Think of three jobs that you would like to do in the future. Explain the reasons for your choices.

UNIT 12

VOCABULARY

Common verbs & collocations

1 Work in pairs. Choose the best word in the box to complete each of the sentences.

> bus   shower   job   notes   shopping   rest

1 Whose turn is it to do the ....? Come on, I cooked.
2 I didn't make .... during the lecture and now I can't remember anything.
3 If you have a short .... every couple of hours, it can help you work better.
4 I need to have a .... in the morning or I can't wake up!
5 You did a very good .... with that project, it got 10 out of 10.
6 If I take the .... in the morning, I get to work at a good time.

2 a Write the correct form of *do* or *make* to complete the sentences.

1 I .... some volunteer work in my year off.
2 I'd like to .... a lot of money before I die.
3 I like .... lists, it's a good way to organise my life.
4 I hate .... phone calls, I prefer to speak to someone face to face.
5 I .... a lot of sports at school, but not now.
6 I never .... the housework or the cooking at home, I'm very lazy.

b 💬 Work in pairs. Tell your partner if the sentences are true for you.

I wouldn't like to make a lot of money, but a good living is OK!

Describing places

3 Which of the nouns in the box can you see in the photos on page 130?

> lakes   architecture   hotels   airport   hills
> transport   trees   mountains   shops

4 Think of any positive adjectives which can combine with the nouns in 3.

5 💬 Work in pairs. Use the phrases in 4 to describe a place you know well.

GRAMMAR

Present perfect & past simple

1 Write the words in the correct order.

1 to Italy ever Have you been ?
2 office you Have worked an ever in ?
3 met famous you a ever person Have ?
4 read Have ever English book a you in ?
5 Have done really ever exciting you something ?
6 flown the you Have across ever Atlantic ?

2 💬 Ask and answer the questions in pairs. When the answer is *yes*, give more information.

Yes, I have. I went to Sicily two years ago.

Review of verbs

3 a Complete the questions with the correct form of the verbs.

1 When .... (begin) to study English?
2 How often .... (have) English classes?
3 Who .... (be) your first English teacher?
4 What .... (can) do well in English?
5 What .... (find) difficult about it?
6 What .... (want) to improve?
7 Where .... (study) English next year?
8 .... ever .... (visit) an English-speaking country?

b 💬 Work in pairs. Ask your partner the questions and report back to the rest of the class.

FUNCTIONAL LANGUAGE

Finding out & recommending

1 a Match the questions to the answers.

1 What's Ibiza like?
2 Can you recommend a hotel for us there?
3 Have you ever been to the Balearic Islands?

a Yes, they're beautiful. I've been lots of times.
b You'll find it very busy in the summer. June or September are good months to go.
c Try the Marina Suites hotel in Ibiza Town. You'll love it!

b 🔊R17 Put the questions and answers in the correct order. Listen and check your answers.

2 💬 Work in pairs. Practise recommending places to go on holiday with your partner.

◼ LOOKING BACK

- Which section of this unit do you think is the most memorable?
- Think of five useful phrases from this unit you can use tomorrow.
- Think of five things you can say to describe your experiences and achievements.

138

Bring it together 10, 11 & 12

Review D

Reading

1 a Read the students' answers to their teacher's homework question. Which students talk about
1 a past experience?   2 future plans?   3 English at work?

Do you use English outside the classroom?
Homework task, 9 July

Javi says
My company does a lot of business with companies in Central Europe. We always communicate in English. Sometimes it's really difficult.

Montse says
I use English a lot online. It's really easy to make friends – from all over the world! We chat about stuff and send photos and videos.

Marisa says
There are a lot of tourists and visitors in my town in the summer. I sometimes speak to them on the street. They ask me for directions.

Lin says
Last year I went to Poland on holiday. It was great. I spoke a lot of English!

Guido says
I don't really use English much outside the classroom ☹ – I hope to start a language exchange with someone who wants to learn Italian.

Elena says
I've never been to an English-speaking country, but this year I'm going to visit my brother in Australia. I really need to improve my English before I go!

Jordi says
I work in a bar. Sometimes people come in and ask for something in English. Sometimes we chat about where they come from and what they're doing in town.

b Read the answers again. Which students do you think use English most?

2 Write your answer to the teacher's question. Compare with a partner. Which student is most similar to you?

Speaking

3 a Answer the questions for yourself.
1 Have you ever visited an English-speaking country?
2 Have you ever visited a country where you needed to communicate in English?
3 Have you ever met an English-speaking person in your home town?
4 Have you ever spoken English with a visitor to your town?
5 Have you ever used English to speak to friends online?

b Work in pairs. Compare your answers and discuss your experiences. Also discuss any questions you answered 'No' to.

Would you like to visit an English-speaking country? Which one?/Why not?
How can you find people to talk to in English in your town?

Quick check

Complete the checklist below.

Can you...	Yes, I can.	Yes, more or less.	I need to look again.
1 talk about future plans?	☐	☐	☐
2 make predictions?	☐	☐	☐
3 talk about past experiences?	☐	☐	☐
4 make offers and requests?	☐	☐	☐
5 compare jobs and work conditions?	☐	☐	☐
6 compare and discuss options?	☐	☐	☐
7 give instructions?	☐	☐	☐
8 make recommendations?	☐	☐	☐

Compare your answers with a partner.
- What else do you know now after studying units 10–12?
- Do you need to look again at any of the sections?
- Do you need any extra help from your teacher?

Unit 7 Grammar reference

7.1 Past simple: *to be*

+	I/He/She/It was You/We/They were	very happy.
−	I/He/She/It wasn't (was not) You/We/They weren't (were not)	very happy.
?	Was I/he/she/it Were you/we/they	happy?
Y/N	Yes, I/he/she/it was. Yes, you/we/they were.	No, I/he/she/it wasn't. No, you/we/they weren't.

We often use *was/were* with *there*.

Use *was* to talk about single things:
Was there a swimming pool?
There wasn't a swimming pool, but there was a beach.

Use *were* to talk about more than one thing:
Were there a lot of tourists?
No, there weren't. There were local families and lots of children.

▶ 7.1

7.2 Past simple: regular & irregular verbs

We use the past simple to talk about actions that happened in the past.

Most verbs have a regular past form. With regular verb forms in the past simple we add *-ed* to the infinitive.

We use *didn't* to form negative verbs and *did* to form questions.

+	I/You/We/They He/She/It	missed		the bus.
−	I/You/We/They He/She/It	didn't	miss	the bus.
?	Did	I/you/we/they he/she/it	miss	the bus?
Y/N	Yes, No,	I/you/we/they/he/she/it		did. didn't.

Spelling rules

1 When a verb ends in consonant–vowel–consonant, double the final consonant and add *-ed*: *stop* → *stopped*
2 When a verb ends in *-e*, drop the *-e* and add *-ed*: *dance* → *danced*
3 When a verb ends in consonant + *y*, change the *-y* to *-i* and add *-ed*: *try* → *tried*
4 When a verb ends in vowel + *y*, simply add *-ed*: *play* → *played*

Irregular verbs

Some verbs have an irregular past simple form in the affirmative. Here are some common irregular verbs:
do → *did*, *go* → *went*, *have* → *had*

▶ 7.2

7.3 Uses of the past simple

We also use the past simple to talk about:

1 specific events in the past: *Yesterday I played football.*
2 habits and routines in the past: *I took the bus to school when I was younger.*
  (= I did this every day, not just on one specific occasion.)

▶ 7.3

7.1

a Choose the correct form of the verb. Then decide if the sentences are true or false.

1 There *was* / *were* a wall between East Berlin and West Berlin before 1989. T / F
2 Tokyo, Vienna and Sydney *was* / *were* all Olympic cities. T / F
3 Rio de Janeiro *was* / *were* once the capital of Brazil. T / F
4 The Vikings *was* / *were* from Scandinavia. T / F

b Order the words to make questions. Then answer the questions.

1 born / you / were / where ?
2 name / the / what / of / your / primary / school / was ?
3 you / at / home / last / night / were ?
4 with / your / family / you / were ?

7.2

Read about Leona's weekend. Six of the verbs in bold are incorrect. Find and correct the mistakes.

First I **goed** to the doctor's on Friday morning and everything was fine. After that I **tryed** to get a haircut, but the hairdresser's was closed. That was bad luck. Then I **haved** my English class. It was great and I **talked** a lot in English. I think I'm improving. The class **finished** at ten, so I **went** for a drink with the other students. On Saturday I **played** tennis with my friend Luke. In the afternoon I **chated** with some friends on the internet. I **didn't want** to go out, so I **stayed** in and **watchd** TV. In the evening I **went** for dinner at the Capri with Gloria. Sunday was quiet. I **didn't did** anything until the evening, when I **had** a date at the theatre. After the show, I was really tired – what a weekend!

7.3

a Write three sentences about what you did yesterday.

1 ....
2 ....
3 ....

b Write three sentences about things you did every day when you were at primary school.

1 ....
2 ....
3 ....

146

UNIT 8

GRAMMAR REFERENCE

8.1 PAST SIMPLE: IRREGULAR VERBS

Here are more common verbs that have an irregular form in the past simple:

give → gave	read → read /red/	speak → spoke
leave → left	say → said	think → thought
make → made	send → sent	write → wrote
meet → met	sit → sat	

Remember that in questions and negatives, we use *did/didn't* and the infinitive:

*What did she **write** about?*
NOT *What did she ~~wrote~~ about?*
*She didn't **speak** about our interests.*
NOT *She didn't ~~spoke~~ about our interests.*

Past simple: time expressions

Here are some common time expressions we use with the past simple:

• *in* + year: *in 1966*

• *at* + age: *at the age of 16*

• *during* + period of time: *during his career*

• *on* + day: *on his birthday, on the day he died*

▶ 8.1

8.2 VERB + *TO* + INFINITIVE

Here are some common verbs that are always followed by *to* + infinitive:

• decide: *We decided to go to the party.*

• hope: *She's hoping to go to university next year.*

• plan: *They're planning to buy a new house.*

• want: *I want to watch the football.*

• would like: *I'd like to see a film tonight.*

▶ 8.2

8.3 SEQUENCERS

We use sequencers to show the order of events and actions in a story. Here are some common sequencers and their uses:

• *first* or *at first*: to introduce the initial event or action in a series

• *then*: to introduce the events or actions that follow

• *later*: to explain that an event or action happened some time after the others

• *finally* or *in the end*: to talk about the end of the story

▶ 8.3

8.1

a Complete the sentences with one negative and one positive form of the verb in brackets.

1 Agatha Christie *didn't write* romances, she *wrote* crime novels. (*write*)

2 Hadrian _____ 'Veni, vidi, vici,' Caesar _____ it. (*say*)

3 Cromwell _____ America, Columbus _____ it. (*discover*)

4 People _____ emails in the past, they _____ letters. (*send*)

5 People _____ e-books in the past, they _____ paper books. (*read*)

6 People _____ a partner online in the past, they _____ in person. (*meet*)

b Choose the correct preposition to complete the sentences. Then change the sentences so they are true for you.

1 I started school *at / on* the age of seven.

2 I was born *in / on* 1992.

3 I went to Norway *at / during* the summer holidays.

4 I went to the cinema *at / on* my birthday.

8.2

Order the words to make sentences. Are these statements true about you?

When I was a kid...
1 hoped / famous / I / be / to / one day
2 make / a lot of money / planned / to / I

Now that I'm older...
3 happy / want / I / have / life / to / a
4 better / like / a / be / I'd / to / person

8.3

Complete the story using *finally, later, at first* and *then*.

I always wanted a large house and lots of money, so I married a rich man. _____ we were very happy. _____ my husband lost his job. _____ we lost the house, the car and all our money! But we still had each other. _____ I understood that money isn't everything!

147

UNIT 9 GRAMMAR REFERENCE

9.1 COUNTABLE & UNCOUNTABLE NOUNS

Countable nouns can be singular or plural:
an egg/some eggs
a cake/some cakes

Uncountable nouns are always singular:
some toast with butter and jam

We can't use *a/an* or numbers with uncountable nouns:
~~a butter~~
~~one butter~~

A/An & some

	Singular	Plural
Countable nouns	a/an a banana an egg	some some tomatoes
Uncountable nouns	some some milk some rice	

1 Some nouns can be both countable (C) and uncountable (U), e.g. *coffee*:

C: *I had a coffee for breakfast.* (= a cup of coffee)

U: *Coffee is good for you.* (= coffee in general)

2 Some words are uncountable in English but countable in other languages, e.g. *toast*. We say:

some toast, a piece of toast, a slice of toast, NOT ~~a toast~~.

▶ 9.1

9.2 QUANTIFIERS

We use quantifiers to talk about quantity:

- *How much/many...?* = asking a question about quantity
- *too much/too many* = more than you need or want
- *a lot of/lots of* = a large quantity
- *some* = a part of something but not all
- *a little/a few, not much/not many* = a small quantity

Notice which ones we use with uncountable nouns and which with countable nouns:

Uncountable nouns	How much (butter)? too much/a little/not much (milk)
Countable nouns	How many (bananas)? too many/a few/not many (tomatoes)
Both uncountable & countable	a lot of/lots of/some (rice/biscuits)

▶ 9.2

9.1

Match the labels, 1–6, to the photos, a–f. Then choose the best word to complete the labels.

1 *a /* (some) water   d   4 *a / some* rice _____
2 *a / an* apple _____   5 *a slice of / a* bread _____
3 *a / some* coffee _____   6 *some / an* onions _____

a   b

c   d

e   f

9.2

Complete the statements with the words in the boxes. Do you agree with what the people say? Why/Why not?

    a few   how much   lots of   much

(1) _____ salt and sugar do I eat? I don't use (2) _____ salt. I think it's bad for you. The problem is I love sugary foods. Chocolate is my favourite. I eat (3) _____ chocolate! I try to eat (4) _____ fresh vegetables when I can.

    a lot of   how much   many   much

(5) _____ fruit do you think I need to eat? I eat (6) _____ bananas and apples, but I don't eat (7) _____ exotic fruit. I don't like the taste of mango or papaya, not (8) _____ people do.

148

UNIT 10

GRAMMAR REFERENCE

10.1 COMPARATIVE ADJECTIVES

We use comparative adjectives to compare two things and talk about the difference between them:

The e-reader is lighter than a book.

The form we use depends on the length of the adjective.

One syllable	Two syllables ending in -y	Two syllables or more
Add -er fast → faster	Change -y to -i and add -er easy → easier	Use more + adjective expensive → more expensive

We use *than* with comparative adjectives:

*It's bigger **than** mine.*

Spelling rules for one-syllable adjectives

1 When the adjective ends in -e add -r: *white → whiter*
2 When the adjective ends in consonant–vowel–consonant, double the last letter and add -er: *fat → fatter, big → bigger*
3 Some adjectives are irregular, e.g. *good → better, bad → worse*

▶ 10.1

10.2 GOING TO

We use *be + going to + infinitive* to talk about future plans.

+	I You/We/They He/She/It	'm going to 're going to 's going to	work hard.	
−	I You/We/They He/She/It	'm not going to aren't going to isn't going to	work hard.	
?	Am Are Is	I you/we/they he/she/it	going to	work hard?
Y/N	Yes, I am. Yes, you/we/they are. Yes, he/she/it is.		No, I'm not. No, you/we/they aren't. No, he/she/it isn't.	

▶ 10.2

10.3 PERSONAL PRONOUNS

We use personal pronouns instead of the names of people and things.

Subject pronouns tell us who, or what, the subject of the verb is. They usually come before the verb:

***I**'m going to call Tomas.*

Object pronouns tell us who, or what, the object of the verb is. They come

1 after the verb: *I'm going to call **him**.*
2 after prepositions: *Tomas is going to come with **us**.*

Subject	Object		Subject	Object
I	me		we	us
you	you		you	you
he	him		they	them
she	her			
it	it			

▶ 10.3

10.1

a Choose the best form of the adjective in brackets to complete the sentences.

1 Dogs are _____ (friendlier / more friendly) than cats.
2 Coffee is _____ (more nice / nicer) than tea.
3 English is _____ (easier / more easy) to learn than Chinese.
4 The flu is _____ (badder / worse) than a cold.
5 The mountains are _____ (more good / better) than the beach for a holiday.
6 Trains are _____ (more expensive / expensiver) than planes.

b Do you agree with these statements? Change the ones you do not agree with.

c Look at the sentences in a again. Write a different sentence comparing the two things. Use a dictionary to help you.

Dogs are noisier than cats.

10.2

a Reorder the sentences to write questions using *going to*.

1 What / you / to / going / do / are / tomorrow ?
   What are you going to do tomorrow?
2 going / you / are / do / to / When / some / studying ?
3 What / you / to / are / going / study ?
4 see / your / When / going / to / are / you / friends ?
5 you / watch / going / tonight / Are / to / TV ?
6 are / What / you / to / going / watch ?

b Write true answers to the questions. You can use positive and negative sentences.

10.3

Complete the sentences with subject or object pronouns.

1 This is Annie Leibovitz. I like _____ a lot. _____'s a great photographer.

2 This is my watch. _____'s an old Rolex. My grandfather gave _____ to _____ when I was 10 years old.

3 My brother and I had this bike. _____ rode it when _____ were children. _____ has a lot of happy memories for _____ .

149

UNIT 11 GRAMMAR REFERENCE

11.1 Superlative adjectives

We use superlative adjectives to compare people/things with all the other people/things in a group:

Hairdressers are the happiest profession. (= Hairdressers are happier than all the other professions.)

The form we use depends on the length of the adjective.

One syllable	Two syllables ending in -y	Two syllables or more
Add -est fast → fastest	Change -y to -i and add -est easy → easiest	Use most + adjective expensive → most expensive

We often use *the* or possessive adjectives (*my, your, his*) with superlative adjectives:

*It's **the** best job. She's **my** best friend.*

Spelling rules for one-syllable adjectives

1 When the adjective ends in *-e* add *-st*: *white → whitest*
2 When the adjective ends in consonant–vowel–consonant, double the last letter and add *-est*: *fat → fattest, big → biggest*
3 Some adjectives are irregular, e.g. *good → best, bad → worst*

▶ 11.1

11.2 Will/Won't

We use *will/won't* + infinitive to talk about what we know and think about the future:

I'll be 30 next birthday. (Future fact: I know this is true.)

It'll be a great party. (Prediction: I think this is true.)

+	I/You/He/She/It/We/They	'll (will)	win.
–	I/You/He/She/It/We/They	won't (will not)	win.
?	Will	I/you/he/she/it/we/they	win?
Y/N	Yes, No,	I/you/he/she/it/we/they	will. won't.

We use the contracted form of *will* ('ll) after names and pronouns:

I think Tom will win. → I think Tom'll win.
He will enjoy the job. → He'll enjoy the job.

▶ 11.2

11.3 Will & might

We can use both *will* and *might* to make predictions about the future.

We use *will* to say that we are **sure** something will happen.
We use *might* to say that we think something is **possible**, but we're not sure:

He'll pass all his exams. (I'm sure this is true.)
He might pass all his exams. (This is a possibility, but I'm not 100% sure.)

When we want to ask other people what their opinion is about the future we usually use *will*:

Will there be jobs for them? What will they do?

+	I/You/He/She/It/We/They	might	win.
–	I/You/He/She/It/We/They	might not	win.

▶ 11.3

11.1

a Complete the questions with the superlative form of the adjective in brackets.

1 What's the _____ thing about learning English? *(easy)*
2 What's the _____ thing about learning English? *(difficult)*
3 What's the _____ bar you know? *(good)*
4 What's the _____ city you know? *(interesting)*
5 What's the _____ place in your town? *(busy)*
6 What's the _____ thing about travelling? *(bad)*
7 What's the _____ gadget that you have? *(new)*
8 Which company is the _____ employer in your region? *(big)*

b Answer the questions and explain your answers.

The easiest thing about learning English is the grammar. The grammar in my language is more complicated!

11.2

Write predictions using *will/won't* and the prompts.

1 by 2020 / there / be / food for everybody in Africa
2 my team / win / cup next season
3 the temperature of the planet / increase a lot over the next ten years
4 doctors / find / a cure for cancer in the next ten years
5 I / run a marathon next year

11.3

a Make predictions for the weather where you live using *will/won't* or *might/might not*. Use the vocabulary on page 73 to help you.

1 Tomorrow it _____ .
2 Next weekend it _____ .
3 On my birthday it _____ .
4 Next December it _____ .
5 Next July it _____ .

b Change the predictions for a town/city in another country.

Unit 12

12.1 Present perfect: *have you ever...?*

We use the present perfect to talk about past experiences:
Have you ever been to Argentina? No, I haven't, but I've been to Chile.

We form the present perfect with *have/has* + past participle.

+	I/You/We/They He/She/It	've (have) 's (has)	been to Brazil.
−	I/You/We/They He/She/It	haven't (have not) hasn't (has not)	been to Brazil.
?	Have Has	I/you/we/they he/she/it	(ever) been to Brazil?
Y/N	Yes, I/you/we/they have. Yes, he/she/it has.	No, I/you/we/they haven't. No, he/she/it hasn't.	

Past participles

We form the past participle of regular verbs by adding *-ed* to the infinitive of the verb: *visit → visited*

The spelling rules of regular past participles are the same as the rules for regular past simple affirmative verbs. See page 146.

Some verbs are irregular: *meet → met, see → seen, win → won*

Been/Gone

Go has two past participles, *been* and *gone*. When we use the present perfect to talk about experience, we usually use *been*:
He's been to London. (= He went to London at some time in the past, but he's not there now.)
He's gone to London. (= He went to London at some time in the past and he's still there now.)

▶ 12.1

12.2 Present perfect & past simple

We use the present perfect when we don't give a specific time in the past:
*I've **been** to Rome.* (We don't say when.)

We use the past simple if we say when something happened:
*I went to Zurich **a few years ago**.*

We use the present perfect to ask an initial question about past experiences:
Have you (ever) been to Thailand? Yes, I have.

We use the past simple to ask for more information:
Did you have a good time there? It was OK.

▶ 12.2

12.3 Review of verbs

We use the present simple to talk about things we do regularly:
I go to English class twice a week.

We use the present continuous to talk about what we are doing now:
I'm watching the football.

We use the past simple to talk about what happened at a specific time in the past: *I went to bed late last night.*

We use *going to* to talk about future plans: *I'm going to start a business.*

We use *will* to talk about what we know or think about the future:
Jack will be 6 on Saturday.

We use *can* to talk about ability and permission: *Can you speak Japanese?*

▶ 12.3

Grammar reference

12.1

a Order the letters to make irregular past participles. Then write the infinitive form of the verb.

1 neeb — *been – go*
2 tem
3 konpes
4 tenrwit
5 nlwof
6 nru
7 neod
8 tugaht

b Reorder the words to make questions with the participles in **a**.

1 you / Have / a marathon / run / ever ?
2 father / Has / a letter / ever / your / written / to you ?
3 you / flown / Atlantic / the / Have / across / ever ?
4 to / spoken / Has / your / ever / mother / English / anyone ?
5 done / you / Have / any unusual sports / ever ?
6 taught / you / ever / Have / anything ?
7 met / a / you / ever / Have / person / famous ?
8 of / been / your / family / a / member / to / ever / Australia / Has ?

c Write true short answers to the questions.

1 *Yes, I have./No, I haven't.*

12.2

Choose three questions in 12.1b. Give more information about each one using the past simple.

5 Have you ever done any unusual sports?
Yes, I have. I played a sport called Jorkyball once. It's a kind of football. I played it when I was in Italy. I liked it. It was fun.

12.3

Look at the pictures. Write two or three sentences for each to talk about 1) the past, 2) the present, 3) the future. Make the sentences true for you.

I had a dog when I was a kid, but I don't have one now. I'm not going to buy one because my flat is very small.

WRITING BANK

4 AN EMAIL TO A FRIEND

To: Ulrike
From: Carola
Subject: Hi!

a Hi, Ulrike, thanks for your email! Did you finish your work on time? How was your weekend?

b We had a great time. John loved his birthday present. Thanks for the idea! He knew nothing about it – it was a big surprise. We just told him we wanted to take him out for a special meal – he was really surprised when we arrived at the kayaking centre!

c It was a fantastic day! We did a three-hour trip down the river – all the way to the beach. It's really beautiful there. And the weather was perfect – warm, sunny, no wind. When we got back we had a picnic under the trees. It was really quiet and peaceful – Toni and John went to sleep!

d We really have to do it again soon. Maybe next time you can come, too! How about some time next month? What do you think?

Speak soon,

Carola

1 Read Carola's email to a friend. Why did she write the email?
   1 to invite Ulrike to a party
   2 to thank Ulrike for her birthday present
   3 to tell Ulrike about her weekend

2 Read the email again and answer the questions.
   1 What was John's birthday present?
   2 Who suggested the idea first?
   3 Was it a good idea? Why/Why not?
   4 Does Carola want to go again? How do you know?

3 Work in pairs. Look at the structure of the email. Which paragraph
   1 describes what happened that day?
   2 shows that Carola is answering an email from Ulrike?
   3 invites Ulrike to reply?
   4 tells us the main reason why Carola is writing to Ulrike?

4 a What phrases does Carola use to begin and end her email? What other phrases can you use?

   b Look at the phrases in the box. Which go a) at the beginning, b) at the end of an email?

   Great to hear from you!   Hope all's well with you.
   Keep in touch!   How's it going?   Take care!   Bye for now.

5 Answer the questions about the email.
   1 Are the sentences long or short?
   2 What is the dash (–) used for? Can you use dashes like this in your language?
   3 Which tense is used in the email? Where does this change?

6 Write an email to a friend describing something you did last week.

TIP

When you write an email to a friend, always start with a personal question or comment. Use paragraphs to separate the different sections. Use simple sentences in an informal style. Remember to finish the email with a friendly ending!

WRITING BANK

5 A REPLY TO A BLOG POST

1 Read the blog post. What help does the writer need?

Recently a friend asked me for some advice. She had some visitors for the weekend. She wanted to take them out to eat somewhere special – somewhere they could eat some really nice, typical local food. I suggested a restaurant next to the market in the centre of town. They serve fresh fish from the market there. It's one of my favourite places. My friend agreed – she loves it, too. But the problem was that one of her visitors was a strict vegetarian and the other didn't like fish!

We live in a seaside town, and most of the best restaurants serve fish. The ones that don't serve fish, serve meat! There aren't really any vegetarian restaurants. We looked in the phone book, we looked online… no luck! Does anybody out there have any ideas?

Tags food vegetarians local restaurants comments (3)

2 a Read the post again. What was the writer's suggestion? Why wasn't it a good suggestion?

b Read the comments and answer the questions.
1 Is Tan's suggestion a good one?
2 Why/Why not?
3 Why does Kelly write two replies?

Comments

Tan says How about this? The Banana Tree Café. A new Asian restaurant that opened two weeks ago. It serves fish, but it also specialises in vegetarian meals. The food's great, the prices are good, the atmosphere is very relaxed and it's open seven days a week.

Kelly says Thanks, we'll try it and let you know.

Kelly says Thank you so much, Tan! My friend tried it with her visitors. They loved it! It's now one of my favourite restaurants, too ☺

3 Read the blog post and comments again. Underline all the adjectives. What do they describe? Are they positive or negative?

4 a Work in pairs. Imagine that the blog writer lives in your town. Discuss which restaurants you can recommend and decide on the best one.

b Write a short reply to the blog post. Suggest a place to eat and say why you think it's a good option. Remember to use adjectives in your description.

5 Exchange replies with another pair. Write a comment back to them. Continue exchanging comments until you have nothing left to say.

TIP

When you add a comment or reply to a blog post, use simple language and keep the comment short and to the point. If you are the blog writer, remember to thank people for their comments.

Writing bank

6 A reply to an online advert

1 Read the email. Which advert (a–d) is Ana answering? What are the other adverts about?

Subject: Advert

Hi,

I saw your advert in Small Ads. I'd like to know where the next meeting is, please. And do I need to pay anything or is it free?

Thank you,

Ana

a Amazing studio flat in Cricklewood
You must see it! Email me on flatsearch@flatsandco.com
Ref: XY425

b I'm driving from London to Rome at the beginning of August.

Anyone want to share the driving and the expenses?

Email me on *rosa89@gomail.net*

c Want to practise your English?

Join us at the Language Exchange. We meet every Thursday evening at 8 p.m. for a drink and a chat. Email languageexchange@gomail.net to find out where the next meeting is.

See you there!

d 3 for 1 computer games

Do you have any games you don't play anymore? Why not bring them to us!

Three second-hand games get you one brand new game of your choice.

3for1@oldfornew.com

2 Read the email again and answer the questions.
1 Which descriptions match Ana's email best?
   a short and direct
   b formal and polite
   c friendly and polite
   d formal and distant
2 What does Ana's email **not** do? Tick the options.
   a give information about herself
   b ask for more information about the Language Exchange
   c arrange a time to meet
   d thank the person she's writing to
   e explain where she saw the advert

3 a Imagine you are interested in two of the other adverts. Write short, polite emails asking for more information.

b Show your emails to a partner. Can he/she guess which adverts you're answering?

4 a Read the reply to Ana's email. Does it answer all her questions?

Subject: Meeting place

Hi Ana,

We're meeting at the Cactus Café on New Street, next to the old theatre. There's no fee to pay, but all members buy their own food and drink.

Hope to see you on Thursday!

Stefan

b Write similar replies to your partner's emails in 3a.

Tip

Remember to make your emails short, clear and to the point. They do not need to be formal. They should have a polite but friendly tone.

COMMUNICATION BANK

4.1 Grammar, page 41, Exercise 5

4.5 Writing task, page 47, Exercise 3

4.2 Grammar, page 43, Exercise 5

COMMUNICATION BANK

5.5 Speaking task, page 57, Exercise 7

Read the extra information about Nia and her family. Underline the important information. Compare your notes on the two interviews. Then decide who is the best childminder for her, and why.

Nia Thomas

We live in a big house in the country. It's 10 km to the nearest town. There's no public transport. A car or bike is essential. The childminder can use our car if necessary. The boys have bikes and they love cycling. There are lots of good places to cycle near the house. I don't want the boys to watch TV or play computer games during the day. In the morning the boys do two hours of schoolwork – reading, writing, Maths and Spanish. Jake has judo lessons twice a week and Josh plays the guitar. They need to practise every day. We have a swimming pool in the garden. The boys can swim, but need an adult with them at all times. We have three big dogs. They love playing with the boys. I do all the cooking and cleaning, but sometimes I need help with the shopping.

REVIEW B, page 68, Grammar, Exercise 4

REVIEW B, page 69, Functional language, Exercise 1

Student A

Act out a phone conversation. Call student B and ask to speak to Joy. You want to talk to her about a game of tennis. You want to change the time to 6.30 p.m.

11.3 Speaking, page 123, Exercise 3

Student B

Think of three questions to ask a fortune-teller about each of these topics:

love, life, health, holidays, work

REVIEW B, page 71, Reading & Speaking, Exercises 1–2

8.5 Writing task, page 91, Exercise 5

Student A

The summer redneck* games take place every year in July in East Dublin, Georgia, USA. The first games took place in 1996, the same year as the Olympics in Atlanta, Georgia. The games were a comic version of the official Olympics. They were a great success. Five thousand people came to the first games. There were lots of strange competitions, including diving into mud (see photo on page 91). The games still take place every year and thousands of people come to watch and compete.

* *redneck* = a working-class white person from the southern states of the USA

9.3 Listening & Reading, page 98, Exercise 1b

159

COMMUNICATION BANK

9.4 Functional language, page 100, Exercise 6

Students A and B, you are the customers. Student C, you are the waiter. Act out the scene using the menu below.

PIZZA PALACE

STARTERS

Asparagus
The finest asparagus with fresh Parmesan cheese and extra virgin olive oil.

Antipasto
A choice of cured Italian meats, served with baked ciabatta, rocket, rustica tomatoes and Parmesan cheese.

MAINS

Margherita
Mozzarella and tomato: pure and simple.

American
Nothing but a big helping of pepperoni for those who love their flavours strong and simple.

Four Seasons
Four pizzas in one: mushrooms, pepperoni, mozzarella, olives, anchovies and capers.

Pollo Siciliano
Chicken in a rich tomato sauce, served on a bed of rice.

DESSERTS

Tiramisu
Italian for 'pick me up': espresso coffee, cocoa, rich cream, mascarpone and Marsala sponge.

Fragole Fresche
Fresh strawberries topped with a blend of honey and fresh yoghurt.

REVIEW C, page 103, Functional language, Exercise 2

Student A
Tell student B your news. Take turns responding to each other's news.

> I passed the exam. I got an A.

> Dad bought a new car last week.

> I left my bag on the train!

> Helen wrote me an email last week. She's in Australia!

10.1 Grammar, page 109, Exercise 4

Look at the pairs of pictures and answer the questions.
1 What's the difference between the two items?
2 Which item do you prefer in each pair? Why?

a

b

c

160

COMMUNICATION BANK

10.2 Speaking, page 110, Exercise 2

Read the survey questions. Answer them with *always*, *sometimes* or *never*. Who is the most dependent on their mobile phone in your group? Why?

You and your mobile

1. Do you send more than 15 texts a day?
2. Do you use your mobile like a radio in public places?
3. If you get a missed call, do you phone back immediately?
4. Do you make calls instead of texting, even if it's an expensive time or it's long distance?
5. Do you look at your mobile first thing when you wake up?
6. If you're at a concert, do you leave your phone on silent and take photos with it?
7. If you leave your mobile at home, do you go back home to get it?
8. Do you text or make calls when you're bored?
9. Do you get anxious if a person doesn't respond to your call or text at once?
10. Do you ever turn off your mobile? When?

11.1 Speaking & Listening, page 119, Exercise 3b

1. **The five worst-paid jobs in the UK (with salaries of less than £10,000 a year):**
   call centre workers, cleaners, fast-food restaurant staff, hairdressers, school cooks

2. **The five best-paid jobs in the UK (with salaries of over £1,000,000 a year):**
   bankers, best-selling writers, celebrities, footballers, lawyers

3. **The five most stressful jobs in the UK:**
   air traffic controllers, inner-city teachers, junior doctors, miners, police officers

11.3 Speaking, page 123, Exercise 3

Student A

Think of three predictions that student B might want to hear about these topics:

love, life, health, holidays, work

Then answer student B's questions.

REVIEW B, page 69, Functional language, Exercise 1

Student B

Act out a phone conversation. Student A calls you and asks to speak to Joy. Explain that Joy isn't in, she's at a music lesson. Take a message.

8.5 Writing task, page 91, Exercise 5

Student B

In a small village in Gloucestershire*, south-west England, a strange event happens every year: a cheese-rolling competition. Last year thousands of people took part. The event is hundreds of years old. It takes place on the last Monday in May. The event consists of a number of races down a very steep hill. At the start of each race, a local celebrity rolls a cheese down the hill. The racers run after the cheese. The first person to reach the bottom of the hill is the winner. The winner gets... guess what... the cheese they ran after, of course!

* Gloucestershire is famous for its rich red cheese.

9.0 page 92, Exercise 2

The photo shows the food an average family wastes every month.

REVIEW C, page 103, Functional language, Exercise 2

Student B

Tell student A your news. Take turns responding to each other's news.

> I failed my driving test – again! That's the fifth time!

> My parents are buying a new house – with a swimming pool!

> Sorry, I can't play tennis with you tomorrow.

> The school is offering free English classes in the morning.

SELECTED TRANSCRIPTS

7.2, *p. 73, Ex 5*

Let's take a look at the weather today in the South America region. It's very hot, dry and sunny in Paraguay, with a maximum temperature of 35 degrees in the capital Asunción. It's a **cool**, wet day in São Paulo. It's raining, with a maximum temperature of 15 degrees centigrade. It's **warm** and sunny in Montevideo, with an expected high of 21 degrees. Meanwhile, it's a windy day in Buenos Aires with the maximum temperature a cool 12 degrees there. As for tourist spots, it's not a good day for the beach in south Brazil. It's raining in Florianópolis with a temperature of only 17 degrees. For those of you who are visiting the glaciers in El Calafate, it's snowing and the temperature is only just above **freezing** ... it's showing a very cold 1 degree centigrade at the moment – a very **cold** and icy day in this part of Patagonia. In the north of Argentina, on the border with Brazil, it's still warm. At Iguazu Falls there's a pleasant high of 23 degrees, but it's cloudy and humid.

7.4, *p. 76, Ex 2*

P = Patti   L = Lola

P: How was the beach?

L: Oh, it was a total disaster!

P: Disaster? What do you mean?

L: Well, first of all, we arrived there and within, like, ten minutes it started to rain ... and I mean really rain!

P: Yeah, I remember. That was quite a storm at the weekend! So, what did you do?

L: Well, to start with, we waited in one of the beach cafés ... you know ... for the rain to stop, or something. We

had a coffee, we played a couple of games of cards ... but it didn't stop, it just rained ... and rained ... and rained. So in the end we decided to go home.

P: Yeah?

L: Yeah ... well, we walked to the road, to the bus stop, but just as we reached it ... there was the bus, far away in the distance! We were too late ... we missed the bus and there wasn't another one for two hours!

P: Oh, no!

L: Oh, yes! We didn't want to wait for the bus in the rain, so we walked...

P: What? All the way home?

L: Yes, all the way home...

P: Did you call a taxi?

L: No, we didn't. I wanted to ... but hey, it was too expensive ... we didn't have any money.

P: So what did you do when you finally got home?

L: We changed out of our wet clothes, had hot showers ... and then we went out for a pizza and a movie!

P: A much better idea in the rain!

7.7, *p. 78, Ex 1*

1   Bruno

I went to work by subway for years because I lived and worked in Rio. Now I work in São Paulo and Rio, so I go to work by plane. There's an air shuttle every half an hour and I can take any plane I like. I don't travel like this every day, of course. When I go to São Paulo, I normally stay for three or four nights, so it's easy enough. The plane trip is only one hour. I hated flying before, but now it's OK.

2   Erykah

Before, we walked to school, me and my friends – 3 km there and 3 back. We didn't have a choice, because the roads were not in good condition ... or there weren't any roads. Now the roads are better, and there's a school bus that picks us up from the main square in the village. My life changed overnight. It was hard going everywhere on foot...

3   Carole

I went to work by car, I admit it. A single person in a big family car! I like driving, but it's not very good for the environment. I realised one day that this was terrible, so I decided to make some changes. I talked to two friends who live near me and we decided to share

164

Selected transcripts

a taxi together in the mornings. It costs more or less the same and we don't cause so much pollution. The problem is the taxi driver is not always very friendly.

4 Alek

I always went to college by train. It was quite comfortable and there weren't many delays. Then I changed my mind about it because the council introduced a new bike service. The idea is great, but there are always problems. The bikes are sometimes broken, or there aren't any when you want one ... or there isn't any space to leave them. And on rainy days...! Well, it was expensive, but I preferred the train!

🔊 7.9, p. 80, Ex 2

1 A: Excuse me, are you going to the stadium?
   B: No, you need the number 2 bus. The stop's over there, next to the petrol station.

2 A: Excuse me, this ticket machine is out of order. Is there another one?
   B: No, I'm afraid there isn't. You need to go to the ticket office.

3 A: Hi! Can you take me to the airport, please?
   B: Yeah, sure. Which terminal?
   A: Just a second ... erm ... Terminal 4, please...
      ...Thanks, that's great. How much is it?
   B: That's £15.85, please.

4 A: Excuse me, how long does it take to get to the airport by train?
   B: About 35 minutes. There's a train every half an hour.
   A: And by bus?
   B: The bus takes about an hour. It leaves every hour on the hour, from the bus stop over there.
   A: Thanks!

5 A: Oh, no! We just missed the last ferry! When's the next one?
   B: I don't know. Let me check the timetable ... There's another one in 40 minutes.
   A: Why don't we have a coffee while we wait?
   B: Yeah, look there's a bar over there.

🔊 8.5, p. 86, Ex 3

Latest news on the hour every hour. It's nine o'clock and here are tonight's headlines for English speakers in Buenos Aires.

Fears about the new flu pandemic are increasing. Today, the authorities decided to check all passengers entering the country's main airports. Doctors suspect that 11 soldiers in the Argentinian army have the virus. Hospitals are on alert in major cities such as Cordoba, Mendoza and Rosario.

And now the latest from the Rock in the Park festival in Mar del Plata...

Disaster at this year's Rock in the Park as storms hit the coast of Mar del Plata. The country's biggest rock festival is in danger. Last night it rained non-stop and organisers cancelled Friday's concerts. They hope to make an announcement later today about tonight's show with big name bands Depeche Mode and The Killers. Meanwhile, the fans are learning to live with the mud!

Finally, sports news with Clara García...

Thanks, Tom. Yes, amazing but true! They did it ... Lanús won the league last night for the first time in their history, when they beat Vélez Sarsfield, 2–0. José Sand scored both goals to give Lanús victory. Last night, parties continued for hours after the match but the club plan to organise an official party for next weekend.

🔊 8.8, p. 89, Ex 1

Alain Robert is an incredible man – and an incredible climber. He started climbing as a young boy and he climbed his first building at the age of 12. One day he got home, looked in his pockets, but he didn't have his door key. He didn't want to wait for someone to come home, so he decided to climb up the outside of the building – all the way to the eighth floor. This was the beginning of a great passion.

As a young man he had two serious accidents. After the second accident, doctors said that his climbing career was over. But Alain didn't listen to them. He wanted to climb. At first he climbed mountains and then he started to climb towers and famous buildings.

First he climbed the Eiffel Tower in Paris and then the Opera House in Sydney. It is usually impossible to get permission to climb these buildings, so Alain usually starts his climbs in the early hours of the morning, using only his hands and some climbing shoes. And his climbs often end in his arrest! Chinese authorities arrested him in 2007, Brazilian police arrested him in São Paulo in 2008 and British police arrested and fined him when he climbed the Lloyd's building in London in 2009. And so the story continues...

When reporters ask him why he does it, he says what all great climbers say: 'Because I can.' At first he climbed for fun, then he climbed to protest – to protest against his arrests – he really doesn't like authority! – and later to protest about climate change. Some of his climbs were also for money. In 2003 he climbed the Abu Dhabi Bank building to celebrate its opening. Then he climbed the Lloyds building in London in a Spider-Man costume to promote the *Spider-Man* movie. The media started to call him the Human Spider or the French Spiderman.

🔊 8.9, p. 94, Ex 2

1 A: José and Beth moved into their new house last week.
   B: Did they? I didn't know it was ready.
   A: Yeah, I went to see it at the weekend. It's lovely.

2 A: Erika and Kristoff's baby was born last night – at 10 p.m. It's a girl. She's gorgeous!
   B: A girl? That's fantastic news! Kristoff really wanted a girl! What's her name?

3 A: Did you hear about Adam? He lost his job.
   B: Oh, no! When did that happen?
   A: Two days ago. More than a hundred people lost their jobs. The company's in big trouble.
   B: That's awful! I'm really sorry to hear that.

4 A: I passed!
   B: You passed?
   A: Yes, I passed my driving test! Two hours ago!
   B: That's great news! Congratulations!

5 A: Sorry, but I can't come to your party this evening. I've got some work to do.
   B: Oh, no! What a shame! Can't you come later?
   A: Yeah, maybe. I can try, anyway.

🔊 9.2, p. 98, Ex 3

It's sad but true. Every year we throw away one third of the food we buy. That's 6.7 million tonnes of food in the UK. Fruit and vegetables are 40 per cent of this. The top five fruit and vegetables that go

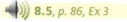

165

SELECTED TRANSCRIPTS

in the rubbish bin are apples, potatoes, bananas, tomatoes and oranges.
But why do we waste so much food? The reason is simple. We buy too much food, we don't use it all and then we throw it away. For example, lots of people forget to put food in the fridge in summer. Obviously, if you put fresh fruit and vegetables in the fridge they stay fresh for longer and you don't need to throw them away.

🔊 10.7, p. 112, Ex 2

P = presenter **FH** = Frederic Hedstrom

P: Welcome to *Buzzword*, the programme that looks at new words, what they mean and how we use them. In the studio today we have Frederic Hedstrom, who is going to talk about flash mobs. What does that mean exactly, Frederic?

FH: Well, a mob is a large group of people, right? And 'flash' suggests speed, something that happens suddenly, something that happens very quickly. Flash mobs are events where big crowds of people meet in a public place and do something together for maybe five minutes ... and then that's it.

P: What's the connection with technology, then?

FH: Well, people know what's happening, and where and when to meet, because they get a text message on their cell phone – or perhaps an email. This means that these events happen very quickly, there's no need to plan in advance. People call, text or send an email and the flash mob takes place only a few hours or minutes later.

P: Yes, I think that's the exciting part of it, they're very spontaneous...

FH: Absolutely.

P: What kind of flash mobs do people organise?

FH: Well, a lot of them are just for fun. There is a very popular one – The Pillow Fight. It takes place all over the world. People get together and fight each other with pillows. That's it. It's silly but great fun!

P: How many people are we talking about here?

FH: More than 5,000 in the New York pillow fight. That's the biggest flash mob ever, bigger than London's silent disco.

P: Silent disco? What's that?

FH: A silent disco – or rave – is when a lot of people meet in a public

place, listen to music on their iPods and dance. It looks really strange. Everybody's dancing, but you can't hear any music! That's why it's called a silent disco – or rave!

P: It all seems very silly. Aren't there any serious flash mobs?

FH: Well, one famous event happened in 2009. Dani Jarque, a footballer and captain of the football club Espanyol in Barcelona, died suddenly at the age of 26. Fans of the club organised a meeting to pay their respects to him. Thousands of people phoned, or sent text messages, like a chain ... and they all met in the same place to light candles and leave flowers.

P: Where did they meet?

FH: At gate 21 of Espanyol's stadium.

P: Why was that?

FH: Because Jarque's shirt number was always 21.

P: I see ... Finally, what's your favourite flash mob, Frederic?

FH: Oh, something silly! There was a No Pants Day in New York. A lot of people got on the subway without their trousers ... it was very funny ... and it was a cold day, too!

🔊 10.10, p. 114, Exs 3 & 4

1 **A:** Oh, no!
   B: What's up?
   A: I don't have any battery!
   B: Use my phone if you want. Here.
   A: Thanks! What do I do?
   B: Key in the number and then press the button with the green phone.
   A: OK. Thanks!

2 **A:** Hey, is that a new phone?
   B: Yeah.
   A: It's the same as mine.
   B: Really? Hey, maybe you can help me. I want to send a photo, but I don't know how.
   A: It's easy! Look, click on 'menu' ... here, see?
   B: Yes...
   A: Then select 'camera', here in the corner...
   B: No, I don't want to *take* a photo, I want to *send* one. Look, here's the photo ... but I don't know how to send it.
   A: Let's see ... oh, yes, click here – see where it says 'more'? Now select 'send'.
   B: OK, now I get it. Thanks!
   A: No problem!

3 **A:** Do you have the time?
   B: Yeah. Look, there's my phone, on

the table.
   A: But it's switched off.
   B: Just press that button on the side.
   A: Which one? This one?
   B: Yes, that's it.
   A: Great! Hey, I like that – my phone doesn't do that!
   B: So what time is it?
   A: Oh, no, ten to six. I'd better go! I don't want to be late!

🔊 11.2, p. 119, Ex 2

A new survey out today says that the five happiest professions in the UK are hairdressers, chefs, priests, plumbers and mechanics. And the five unhappiest are office workers, architects, secretaries, estate agents and bankers. It appears that hairdressers, chefs, priests, plumbers and mechanics have one important thing in common: They make people feel good – or help them solve an important problem – quickly! Which might explain why architects are more unhappy – because it takes a long time to see the results of their work. It can take many years to finish a building, but a haircut or bowl of pasta takes just a few minutes!

🔊 11.3, p. 120, Ex 1

P = Phil **T** = Toni

P: Welcome to Job Search – the radio programme that helps you find your ideal job. Toni, what have you got for us today?

T: Well, Phil, I just saw this incredible job advert on an Australian website. This has to be the best job ever!

P: What is it?

T: Well, the Queensland Tourism Authority is looking for someone to be a caretaker on a tropical island off the coast of Australia – in addition to a fantastic salary of 150,000 Australian dollars...

P: One hundred and fifty thousand?

T: Yes! The caretaker will get 150,000 dollars for a six-month contract. And, in addition to the salary, the caretaker will live rent free – that's right, they won't pay any rent – in a three-bedroom beach-side villa ... with a swimming pool!

P: Wow! That really is the best job ever ... but what will the caretaker need to do?

T: Very little! He or she will work about 12 hours a month.

P: A month? Not a day?

T: No, a month. He or she will collect

166

SELECTED TRANSCRIPTS

the mail – you know, letters and packages and things – for the island, and look after some of the hundreds of different fish that live in the sea around the island.

P: Is that it? Are you sure that's all? There's nothing else they need to do?

T: Well, yes … the caretaker will also write a blog about his or her life on the island. He or she will take photos and videos of all the wonderful beaches and fantastic things to do on the island – and all the other tropical islands around.

P: Ah, I see…

T: That will really be the most important part of the job – they want to attract more visitors to these beautiful islands.

P: So, what kind of person are they looking for?

T: Well, the successful candidate will need to know how to swim, snorkel, dive and sail. And, of course, he or she will need to know how to use a computer…

P: And how to take good photos!

T: Yes, and write a good blog!

P: Well, I'll be interested to see who gets the job of the blogging island caretaker!

T: Me, too!

🔊 12.3, p.129, Ex 1

H = Hanna   R = Renata   S = Stephen

H: …I hate these lists…

R: Why? I think they're interesting…

H: Come on, I mean, life isn't a list … it's how you live from day to day that's important – who you are, not the number of things you do. This is just a list of expensive holiday experiences … just another thing to consume.

R: Consume? What do you mean?

H: Well, it's a list of things to spend money on – things you can buy – isn't it? You know, an exotic holiday or skydiving. All these 'before you die' lists say you haven't had a good life – a full life – if you don't do all these exotic – and expensive! – things. And I think that's wrong.

S: Hanna has a point … and this list is a bit stupid. I mean, drive a Formula One car! That's just for kids! Some people think that life is just about driving fast cars, obviously…

H: I know, that's exactly what I mean. But then, looking again, there are some good things on the list, too. I'd love to go whale-watching, for example.

S: Me too!

R: I did that in Argentina a few years ago. It was brilliant.

S: And I've been to Antarctica.

R: Seriously?

S: Yeah, I went last summer. It was amazing. And I'd love to see the Northern Lights. Hanna, you've lived in Finland, haven't you? Have you ever seen the Northern Lights?

H: No, I haven't. We went up to the north once, but we didn't see the lights. I've seen the midnight sun, though … but then, that isn't on the list, is it? So, I suppose it doesn't count!

🔊 12.4, p. 131, Ex 1

1 **Gus**

I've never been to Scandinavia. I've always wanted to go there, so Copenhagen could be interesting to visit, sure. But everybody tells me it's very expensive there … though that obviously doesn't worry the magazine … maybe the journalists have a lot of money! It looks beautiful in the photo, so clean, and the air so fresh, not like where I live. I went to Munich last summer … I wonder if it's similar. I don't know if the cultural life in Copenhagen is so good, but I like the fact that the people are liberal there – they have open minds. So, yes, I would like to go … one day!

2 **Maria**

Well, I don't know why it's this magazine's number one city. I went to Zurich a few years ago, but I didn't like it much. I didn't have a very good time there. It's a very beautiful place and everything runs on time, like the transport, as they say. But it's not a very friendly place … maybe it's just too efficient. I like cities which have more life, more chaos … for me, the atmosphere on the street is the most important thing, and the cultural life. I don't think it's so great in Zurich. I've been to other cities in Europe which I like more … Berlin, for example.

🔊 12.7, p. 132, Ex 4

I = interviewer   K = Klaus

I: Well, Klaus, we've just heard the news. You're going to represent Munich at this year's Ironman World Championship in Hawaii!

K: I can't really believe it, to tell you the truth! I'm very excited indeed.

I: How did you get the place?

K: I was very lucky! It's a lottery – that's the only way they can limit the number of people in the race. To be in the lottery, you need to do a half Ironman event somewhere in the world, that's all.

I: So, some people think you need to be crazy to do this. Is that right?

K: Well, maybe, yes – I'm sure it helps! I started with normal triathlons, like a lot of people, and I realised that I was quite good. I began as a swimmer, really – I swam in competitions when I was a kid. Then some friends told me about triathlons. I did my first one here in Munich five years ago.

I: Which is your favourite of the three sports?

K: I think it's swimming, that's my best sport. Cycling is the worst one, I sometimes get very tired!

I: So, what are your plans now, Klaus? How are you going to prepare for this event?

K: Good question! The training is very difficult. For the next six months, I'm going to follow a very strict programme. On Tuesdays and Thursdays, I swim about 3 km in my local pool. On Fridays I swim another 2.5 km, and I try and swim in open sea, if I can, but that's not easy here in Munich. On Wednesdays, I usually go for a short run, around 10 to 12 km. On Saturdays, I usually do a long bike ride, which right now is about 120 km! Then, on Sundays, I run a longer distance, about 20 km … but all those distances will start to increase. Mondays are usually my day off!

I: What about the climate in Hawaii?

K: That's a problem. Here in Munich it's very cold, but in Hawaii the weather will be hot – and it can be windy, too. I need to be careful! Right now, I'm running with lots of clothes on to prepare myself for the heat.

I: What about the rules?

K: There are a lot! You can't receive help from anyone in the race, except the officials, who can give you food and drink. Also, there's a new rule for the swimming … you can't wear swimsuits made from certain material because they give you an advantage – they help you swim faster.

I: Well, thanks, Klaus, for telling us about the preparations for the race. Good luck and congratulations!

K: Congratulations?! Let's hope I finish first!

IRREGULAR VERBS

INFINITIVE	PAST SIMPLE	PAST PARTICIPLE
be	was, were	been
become	became	become
begin	began	begun
break	broke	broken
bring	brought	brought
build	built	built
buy	bought	bought
choose	chose	chosen
come	came	come
cost	cost	cost
do	did	done
drink	drank	drunk
eat	ate	eaten
fall	fell	fallen
feel	felt	felt
find	found	found
fly	flew	flown
forget	forgot	forgotten
get	got	got
give	gave	given
go	went	gone, been
have	had	had
hear	heard	heard
hold	held	held
keep	kept	kept
know	knew	known
learn	learnt/learned	learnt/learned
leave	left	left
lose	lost	lost

INFINITIVE	PAST SIMPLE	PAST PARTICIPLE
make	made	made
meet	met	met
pay	paid	paid
put	put	put
read /riːd/	read /red/	read /red/
ride	rode	ridden
ring	rang	rung
run	ran	run
say	said	said
see	saw	seen
sell	sold	sold
send	sent	sent
show	showed	shown
sing	sang	sung
sit	sat	sat
sleep	slept	slept
speak	spoke	spoken
spend	spent	spent
stand	stood	stood
swim	swam	swum
take	took	taken
teach	taught	taught
tell	told	told
think	thought	thought
throw	threw	thrown
wake	woke	woken
wear	wore	worn
win	won	won
write	wrote	written

Contents

7	GOING PLACES	*page 42*
8	IN THE NEWS	*page 48*
9	HUNGRY PLANET	*page 54*
	PROGRESS TEST 3, UNITS 7–9	*page 60*
10	STATE OF THE ART	*page 62*
11	A WORKING LIFE	*page 68*
12	LISTMANIA!	*page 74*
	PROGRESS TEST 4, UNITS 10–12	*page 80*
	TRANSCRIPTS	*page 84*
	TRACK LISTING	*page 88*

The **BIG** Picture
ELEMENTARY **B**
Workbook

LEANNE GRAY
MARK LLOYD

Richmond

7 Going places

Vocabulary
The weather

1 a Find 15 weather adjectives in the word search. Each word starts with an <u>underlined</u> letter.

```
F  R  E  E  Z  I  N  G  C  H  R  D  Y  X  A
E  A  F  W  J  L  Q  G  O  L  O  I  Y  R  Y
B  I  J  G  Y  C  L  T  G  V  O  M  C  Y  D
M  N  M  G  D  F  D  E  M  L  B  U  I  P  C
T  Y  G  E  J  Q  X  W  A  Y  S  H  D  L  O
T  O  K  Q  F  Y  T  B  W  J  O  U  N  Y  O
F  E  B  R  W  J  D  R  L  G  Q  W  D  W  L
Y  D  N  I  W  C  O  L  D  X  D  B  K  O  F
S  F  W  T  V  A  F  O  F  Y  O  L  N  N  S
Z  E  D  C  N  Y  S  H  V  H  U  O  A  S  W
U  W  C  P  W  V  N  Z  C  Z  W  T  E  W  Z
F  L  A  Z  A  K  J  N  D  Y  C  W  L  Y  W
I  Y  W  R  W  B  T  R  U  B  A  O  P  Q  K
G  E  D  L  M  T  A  T  K  S  W  A  W  U  N
```

b Which words can you use to describe winter weather? Which words describe summer weather?

2 Complete the sentences using words from **1**. There may be more than one possible answer.

1 It's difficult to walk when it's _windy_ .

2 Children have a lot of fun when it's _____ .

3 Don't forget your umbrella when it's _____ .

4 If it's _____ , eat an ice-cream to stay cool.

5 Be careful where you walk when it's _____ !

6 It can be hard to see when it's _____ .

7 It's often _____ before a storm.

8 Don't hang your clothes out if it's _____ .

Transport

3 Put the letters in the correct order to make transport words. Then put the circled letters in the correct order to make one extra word.

1 SUB — B U S
2 NIRTA
3 IEBK
4 TOAB
5 PELNA
6 FYRER
7 RCA
8 XATI
9 OIROBTEMK
10 MATR
11 WASUYB

S _ _ _ _ _ _

4 Choose the correct option to complete the sentences.
1 I always take the *bus* / *train* to school. It's easy because the stop is at the end of my street!
2 We travelled from Corfu to Italy by *ferry* / *plane*. It was very slow (16 hours!) but it was fun, too.
3 You can hire *bikes* / *scooters* in the city centre now. I think it's a good idea – cycling is a healthy way to travel.
4 I never drive into town because you can't find anywhere to park the *car* / *taxi*.
5 I travel to work on the *tram* / *subway*. I like it because there are good views of the buildings in the city centre.

5 a Complete the quiz with transport words.

① In Mexico City, a _____ is a green Volkswagen Beetle!
② In London, the _____ is called the Underground and in Paris it is called the Métro.
③ Carl Benz is famous for making the first _____ in 1885.
④ The first _____ trip, in 1904, was only five minutes long.
⑤ In Shanghai, you can take a very fast _____ called a 'maglev' from the city centre to the airport.

b 7.1 Listen and check.

BRING IT TOGETHER

6 Complete the blog post with the words in the box.

cloudy ferries ~~plane~~ rainy
sunny taxi tram windy

29 July 2011
Hello from Hong Kong!

The ⁽¹⁾ *plane* journey was OK – I arrived at the airport this morning. Then I got a ⁽²⁾_____ to my hotel. The driver was very friendly and it wasn't expensive. My room is nice, and there's a fantastic view of the harbour (do you like the photo?). I can see the ⁽³⁾_____ on the water, going to all the different islands. Later I want to take the ⁽⁴⁾_____ that goes up Victoria Peak, right to the top. I hope it's not too ⁽⁵⁾_____ when I get there because I want to see the view of the city.

I'm a bit surprised because the weather here isn't hot. Today, it's cloudy and not ⁽⁶⁾_____ at all. The taxi driver said there might be a typhoon tomorrow. This is when it's really ⁽⁷⁾_____ (I'll need my umbrella!) and ⁽⁸⁾_____ – sometimes trees fall over. If there is a typhoon, you can't go outside. I hope the weather's OK because I want to go sightseeing!

43

7

GRAMMAR
Past simple: to be

1 Choose the correct options to complete the description.

FotoFun

03/07/2011

Here we are at the campsite before our hike. Tomas is making coffee – it **(1)** *was* / *were* very early! The campsite **(2)** *were* / *was* quite basic – there **(3)** *were* / *weren't* any showers or anything. But that **(4)** *wasn't* / *was* really a problem – we **(5)** *was* / *were* very happy to be there! The weather **(6)** *was* / *wasn't* quite cold, because we **(7)** *were* / *weren't* so high up in the mountains, but it **(8)** *was* / *were* a really beautiful place.

2 Complete the conversation with the past simple form of the verb *to be*.

A Hi John! Where **(1)** _were_ you last week? **(2)** _____ you ill?
B No, I **(3)** _____ on holiday, in Venice.
A Wow! **(4)** _____ it your first trip to Venice?
B Yes, it **(5)** _____. But it **(6)** _____ my parents' first trip to Venice. It **(7)** _____ their third visit. They love the city!
A I see! **(8)** _____ there a lot of tourists there?
B No, there **(9)** _____, actually. It **(10)** _____ good because in November the city isn't busy.
A That's good. **(11)** _____ it expensive in Venice?
B Yes, it **(12)** _____. But it's a really beautiful place.

Past simple: regular & irregular verbs

3 Complete the sentences with the past simple form of the verbs in brackets.

1 We _played_ football at the park yesterday. (play)
2 I _____ dinner with a friend last night. (have)
3 I _____ shopping yesterday because I _____ some new shoes. (go, need)
4 We _____ to go to the beach on Saturday, but it _____ all day. (want, rain)
5 I _____ to work because the bus was late. (walk)
6 I _____ a lot of sport at the weekend. Now I feel tired! (do)
7 Neil _____ all night to finish his essay. (work)
8 I _____ my new university course last week. (start)

4 Which of the verbs in **2** are regular in the past simple and which are irregular? Complete the lists.

Regular _play,_ _____

Irregular _____

5 Complete the descriptions using the past simple form of the verbs in the boxes.

| be (x2) | go | have | not go | stay | watch |

My weekend **(1)** _was_ very relaxing. On Saturday I just **(2)** _____ at home and **(3)** _____ TV. I **(4)** _____ out because I **(5)** _____ too tired. On Sunday I **(6)** _____ to the gym, then I **(7)** _____ lunch in the park with some friends.

Flora

| be | decide | do | go | not like | play | work |

On Saturday, I **(8)** _____ in my parents' shop. Then I **(9)** _____ to the cinema but I **(10)** _____ the film very much. On Sunday, I **(11)** _____ very tired so I **(12)** _____ to stay at home. I **(13)** _____ some cooking and **(14)** _____ computer games with my boyfriend.

Sara

44

6 Read the descriptions in **5** again. Number the pictures of Flora and Sara in the correct order.

a 3

b

c

Flora

a

b

c

d

Sara

7 a Complete the questions about Flora and Sara using the past simple form of the verbs in brackets.

1. _Did_ Flora _have_ (have) a relaxing weekend?
   Yes, she did.
2. _____ she _____ (go) out on Saturday?
3. _____ Sara _____ (work) at the weekend?
4. _____ she _____ (do) some cooking?
5. _____ she _____ (watch) TV with her boyfriend?

b Answer the questions using short answers.

Uses of the past simple

8 Choose the correct options to complete the questions.

1. A Where (did) / do you live when you were / was younger?
   B Osaka. I lived there for 15 years.
2. A Did you went / go on holiday this year?
   B No, I didn't. I stayed at home.
3. A Why were / was she late this morning?
   B She missed the bus so she walked to the office.
4. A Do / Did you do a lot of sport when you was / were a child?
   B Yes, I did. I played tennis and basketball.

9 Do the answers in **8** describe a specific event in the past (S), or a past habit (H)?

1 _H_   2 ____   3 ____   4 ____

BRING IT TOGETHER

10 Read the diary. Eight of the verbs in **bold** are incorrect. Find and correct the mistakes.

8th October

Today **was** day one of my new English course.
I **goed** to the school this morning for my first
                    went
class. All the teachers and students **was** really
friendly. But I **missd** the bus, so I **was** late…
on the first day! I **was** really embarrassed.
After the class I **went** to town and **doed** some
shopping. I **didn't have** an an umbrella and I
needed to buy one – it **raind** all day today. ☹

9th October

No rain today! It **was** really sunny this morning
so I **walked** to the school – I **didn't went** by
bus. Today I **had** a lesson in the morning and
a lesson in the afternoon. I **was** really tired
afterwards! But my friends from the school
decided to go out after class. We **haved** dinner
in a great restaurant and then we **went** to the
cinema. The film **was** in English!! It **weren't**
easy to understand but… it **was** fun. I'm back
home now – bed soon!

45

FUNCTIONAL LANGUAGE Using public transport

a ___ b ___ c _1_ d ___ e ___

1 Find and correct one mistake in each sentence. Match the sentences to photos a–e.

1 Oh no! We just miss̸ed the train. When's the next one?
2 Hi, this ticket machine is not the order. Is there another one?
3 Can I have a receive, please?
4 Excuse me, how long it takes to get to the city centre?
5 Hi, can you go me to the station, please?

2 a Match answers f–j to the questions in 2.

f About ten minutes.   _4_
g Yes, of course. Here you are.   ___
h Sure, but which one – bus or train?   ___
i There's another one in about an hour.   ___
j No, you need to go to the ticket office over there.   ___

b 🔊 7.2 Listen and check.

LISTENING Background knowledge

1 Match the places in the box to the photos.

> California   Iceland   Kerala

a _____ b _____ c _____

2 a What do you know about the places in 1? Make notes about the questions.

1 Where are they in the world?
_____

2 What is the weather like?
_____

3 What's the best time of year to visit?
_____

b 🔊 7.3 Listen to three conversations about the places and check.

> **STRATEGY** Sometimes you can use your own knowledge to help you understand difficult listening texts. Before you listen, think about what you know about the topic and ask yourself questions about it.

Key words

3 a Look at the questions and answers. Underline the key words.

1 Why didn't the man like Iceland?
   a There wasn't a lot to do. ☐
   b It was very dark. ☐
2 Why don't they want to go to Kerala in August?
   a You need a lot of money to go there. ☐
   b The weather is very rainy. ☐
3 What did the woman like most about California?
   a The hot weather. ☐
   b The places she visited. ☐

b Listen to the conversations again. Tick (✓) the correct answers.

READING Scanning

1 Read questions 1–3 and match them to replies a–c.

Travel expert Andrew Bell answers your questions

1 **Neil, Manchester**
My wife and I didn't go on holiday in the summer and we want to go somewhere sunny this winter. Can you give us any ideas? _____

2 **Indira, Cardiff**
I want to go on holiday to a Spanish island, but I don't like travelling by plane. What's your advice? _____

3 **Yannis, London**
My job is very busy right now, but in December I can have a few days off. Where can I go for a long weekend? _____

a Why not go to a Christmas market? You can visit a great city like Cologne or Berlin and do your Christmas shopping! The markets have traditional stalls with **handmade** toys and things for the home – you can find a lot of **unusual** presents for your friends and family.

b I suggest Marrakech, in Morocco. I went there in January last year and the weather was great – sunny and warm but not too hot. There's a lot to do: I **explored** the city and did some shopping in the **souks**.

c First, take the Eurostar from London to Paris. Then you can get the Elipsos *trenhotel* to Barcelona. The *trenhotel* has **cosy** bedrooms, a restaurant and a café. **Fares** start at £67 each way. From Barcelona, take a ferry to sunny Ibiza.

2 Answer the questions. Sometimes there is more than one possible answer.

Which reply is helpful if
1 you enjoy train travel? _c_
2 you like warm weather? _____
3 you like shopping? _____
4 you want to go on holiday in winter? _____

Guessing meaning

3 a Look at the words in **bold** in **1**. Match them to the correct type of word, i–iii. Use the questions to help you.

i verb
Is the word after the subject of the sentence (*I*, *we*, etc)? _____
Is it in the past or present tense? How do you know?

ii adjective
Is the word before a noun? _handmade_ _____
Is it similar to an adjective you know (e.g. *friendly* and *unfriendly*)?

iii noun
Is the word at the beginning or the end of a sentence? _____ _____
Is it after an article (*the*, *a*, etc)?

b Match the words to the definitions.
1 adjective: comfortable and warm _____
2 adjective: not usual, different to normal _____
3 noun: a market in an Arab country _____
4 verb, past: to go around a place and look at it _____
5 noun: what you pay for a ticket on a train, etc _____
6 adjective: made by a person, not a machine _handmade_

STRATEGY You can often guess the meaning of words you don't know. Ask yourself questions about the word. Where is the word in the sentence? What type of word is it? Is it similar to another word you know?

8 IN THE NEWS

VOCABULARY

Talking about the news

1 Complete the news words.

1 r a d i o
2 t _ l _ v _ s _ _ n
3 p _ dc _ sts
4 n _ wsp _ p _ r
5 l _ c _ l n _ ws
6 _ nt _ rn _ t
7 b _ s _ n _ ss
8 sp _ rt

2 Complete the text with the words in **1**.

I make sure I read, watch or listen to the news every day. I buy a (1) _newspaper_ every morning and read it while I have my breakfast. I love football, so I always read the articles about (2)_____ at the back. I try to read the (3)_____ section, too – that's useful for work. On my way to the office, I usually listen to the (4)_____ in the car. It's good for (5)_____ about events and things that are going on in my town. But I think the best place to find information is the (6)_____ – there are so many news websites. You can watch videos, listen to (7)_____ , read articles... I hardly ever watch (8)_____ now – I do everything online.

VOCABULARY EXTENSION

Jobs in the media

3 **a** Match the jobs in the box to the descriptions.

cameraman/camerawoman ~~editor~~ journalist
photographer presenter reporter

1 I'm the boss of a newspaper. _editor_
2 I introduce television shows. _____
3 My job is to take pictures for newspapers. _____
4 I appear on news programmes, sending reports about news from around the world. _____
5 I write stories and articles for newspapers and magazines. _____
6 I operate a film or TV camera. _____

b 🔊 8.1 Listen and check.

4 Choose the correct option to complete the sentences.

1 The *cameraman / reporter / photographer* takes great pictures.
2 My mum's *an editor / a journalist / a photographer* – she often interviews politicians for the newspaper.
3 The *presenter / camerawoman / journalist* smiled at the camera and said good night.
4 If you're *a presenter / an editor / a reporter*, you may travel to foreign countries for a news story.

Lexical sets

5 Write the words in the box in the correct group.

~~bands~~ concert doctors festival
goal hospitals league pandemic
score tickets victory virus

___bands___   _____

music

_____   _____   _____

_____   _____   **football**

_____   _____

_____   _____

illness

_____   _____

6 Complete the news stories with the words in **5**.

If you want to buy (1) _tickets_ for next year's Glastonbury music (2)_____ , you're too late! There aren't any tickets left! If you were lucky and have tickets, you'll see famous (3)_____ like Radiohead and The Killers. There is also a big (4)_____ on the last night with a special guest! **1**

(5)_____ are telling their patients to stay at home if they think they have the flu (6)_____ . They think that the (7)_____ might get even worse if people with the virus go to (8)_____ and doctors' surgeries. **2**

Yesterday's match between France and Germany finally ended at 2–1. France were the first team to (9)_____ , but Germany played very well and finished the game with a brilliant, winning (10)_____ in the 89th minute. It was an amazing (11)_____ for the German team – now they can win the (12)_____ if they beat Ireland on Thursday. **3**

7 Match the headlines to the stories in **6**.

a Stop virus spreading _____
b A win in the final seconds _____
c Too late for tickets _____

Collocations

8 Complete the table with the words in the box.

a cold   a concert   a film   the flu   a game of cards   the league
a match on TV   a music festival   the news   a show

get	go to	watch	win
a cold			

9 Complete the conversations with the correct form of the collocations in 8.

1 A What do you want to do on Saturday? Why don't we _go to a show_ ?
  B Hm, I don't really like going to the theatre. How about we _____ at the cinema instead?

2 A Hi Massoud! How are you?
  B Not so good. I _____ last week so I spent the whole weekend in bed.

3 A Did you have a good weekend?
  B Yes, thanks! We _____ . It was great. We saw some really famous bands and it was sunny all weekend.

4 A Hey! How was the football match?
  B Amazing! I love going to the stadium. And our team _____ !

BRING IT TOGETHER

10 Complete the texts with the words in the box.

camerawoman   a concert   a football match   internet   local
news   newspaper   podcasts   presenter   watch

Do you want to work in the media?

Read what three people say about their jobs.

▶ Karin

I'm a sports journalist. I write stories for the sports section of a
(1) _newspaper_ . Some days I'm out all day – I watch (2) _____ at the stadium or I interview a sportsperson. But often my job is a lot less exciting. Just me and my computer! I always use the (3) _____ to find information for my stories.

▶ Max

I'm a (4) _____ on the radio. On my show, we talk about the (5) _____ , about the things that are happening in the world. We sometimes do special programmes about culture and entertainment, so I go to (6) _____ or to a museum about once a week. I think it's great that you can listen to radio programmes on your iPod now – (7) _____ are a really good idea!

▶ Rosa

I'm a (8) _____ for a news programme. I love my job because every day is different – we film stories about (9) _____ news, business and sport. The only problem is that I stand up all day so I'm always really tired in the evening. And I hardly ever (10) _____ the news now – it's too much like work!

8

GRAMMAR
Past simple: irregular verbs

1 Complete the crossword with the past simple form of the verbs.

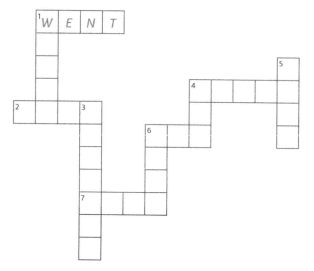

Across
1 go (4)
2 leave (4)
4 speak (5)
6 meet (3)
7 give (4)

Down
1 write (5)
3 think (7)
4 sit (3)
5 read (4)
6 make (4)

2 Complete answers a–h with the past simple form of the verbs in brackets. Match them to questions 1–8.

a Yes, I ___had___ a great time. My friends ___gave___ me some lovely presents! (have, give)
b No, but I _____ him an email. (send)
c They're fine! I _____ to them on the phone yesterday. (speak)
d We _____ each other on our first day at university. We _____ in the same class. (meet, be)
e Yeah, it _____ really nice. We _____ in a café and chatted for hours! (be, sit)
f I _____ , 'Can you come here please?' (say)
g I'm so sorry. I _____ my books at home so I _____ back to get them. (leave, go)
h Not much! I _____ dinner, and then _____ a book. (make, read)

1 What did you do last night? ___h___
2 Why were you late for class this morning? ___
3 How are your parents at the moment? ___
4 Did you have a nice birthday? ___
5 How do you know Luisa? ___
6 Did you call Patrick about the party? ___
7 Did you have a good time with your sister? ___
8 Sorry? What did you say? ___

Time expressions

3 Complete the table with the words and phrases in the box.

| ~~his career~~   2001   the age of 35   14 September |
| my birthday   her life   18 years old   April 1979 |

at	in	on	during
			his career

Verb + to + infinitive

4 Match 1–5 to a–e to make phrases.

1 live   a French
2 study ──────── b a job
3 go   ╲   c abroad
4 watch   d for a walk
5 get   e a film

5 Complete the sentences with the correct form of the verbs and phrases in **4**.

1 If it's sunny this weekend, I'd like ___to go for a walk___ in the mountains.
2 When I'm older, I want _____ . Maybe in Australia!
3 When I finish studying, I hope _____ in a newspaper office. I'm really interested in journalism.
4 We didn't go to the cinema last night. We decided _____ on TV instead.
5 If I pass my exams, I plan _____ at university.

6 Write five sentences about your hopes and plans. Use the ideas in the box.

| at the weekend   in five years   last month |
| on my next birthday   this summer |

50

Sequencers

7 Look at the pictures. Number the notes about Luca's work experience in the correct order, 1–6.

Work experience at *The Evening Times*

___ I enjoyed my week at the newspaper but ⁽¹⁾ _in the end_, I decided that journalism isn't the job for me.

_1_ On Monday, I arrived at the newspaper offices very early. ⁽²⁾ _____ I met Michael, one of the journalists.

___ ⁽³⁾ _____ Michael introduced me to the other people in the office.

___ On Monday, my only job was making coffee!

___ ⁽⁴⁾ _____ I met Marcia the editor of the newspaper. I was really nervous!

___ On Tuesday, Marcia ⁽⁵⁾ _____ gave me some more interesting things to do.

8 a Complete the sentences in **7** using the sequencers in the box.

> finally   first   ~~in the end~~   later   then

b 🔊 8.2 Listen and check.

BRING IT TOGETHER

9 a Read the article. Choose the correct sequencer to complete A–C.

Stories from the streets

John Bird ⁽¹⁾ ___was born___ (be born) in 1946. When he was young, he didn't have a place to live: he was homeless. For a long time, his life was very difficult. ^(A) *Finally / First* he ⁽²⁾ _____ (meet) Gordon Roddick, a businessman. Roddick ⁽³⁾ _____ (have) an idea – he planned ⁽⁴⁾ _____ (start) a 'street paper'. Street papers help homeless people. A person living on the streets can buy the newspaper at a low price and sell it to the public at a higher price. They keep the extra money to help them get a job or find a place to live.

Roddick and Bird hoped ⁽⁵⁾ _____ (help) homeless people in the UK, so in September 1991 they started *The Big Issue*, a British street paper. Now people sell *The Big Issue* all over the world, in countries like Japan, Kenya, South Africa, Malawi and Australia!

Nancy Nikelo worked for *The Big Issue* in South Africa. '^(B) *Later / At first*, when I ⁽⁶⁾ _____ (say) that I wanted ⁽⁷⁾ _____ (sell) *The Big Issue*, people laughed at me. But because I'm a single mother I needed to have an income. I am so happy that I joined the *Big Issue* team.' Selling the newspaper ⁽⁸⁾ _____ (give) Nancy a new start. ^(C) *Then / In the end* she stopped selling *The Big Issue* because she got a full-time job as a teacher.

b Complete 1–8 with the correct form of the verbs in brackets.

51

FUNCTIONAL LANGUAGE Responding to news

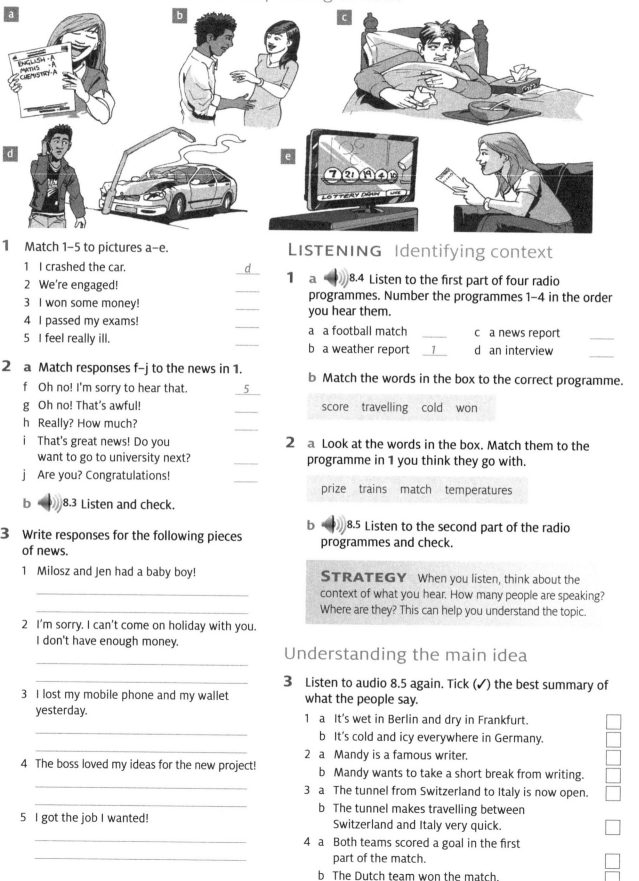

1 Match 1–5 to pictures a–e.
1 I crashed the car. _d_
2 We're engaged! ___
3 I won some money! ___
4 I passed my exams! ___
5 I feel really ill. ___

2 a Match responses f–j to the news in **1**.
f Oh no! I'm sorry to hear that. _5_
g Oh no! That's awful! ___
h Really? How much? ___
i That's great news! Do you want to go to university next? ___
j Are you? Congratulations! ___

b 🔊 8.3 Listen and check.

3 Write responses for the following pieces of news.
1 Milosz and Jen had a baby boy!
   _____
   _____
2 I'm sorry. I can't come on holiday with you. I don't have enough money.
   _____
   _____
3 I lost my mobile phone and my wallet yesterday.
   _____
   _____
4 The boss loved my ideas for the new project!
   _____
   _____
5 I got the job I wanted!
   _____
   _____

LISTENING Identifying context

1 a 🔊 8.4 Listen to the first part of four radio programmes. Number the programmes 1–4 in the order you hear them.
a a football match ___
b a weather report _1_
c a news report ___
d an interview ___

b Match the words in the box to the correct programme.

score   travelling   cold   won

2 a Look at the words in the box. Match them to the programme in **1** you think they go with.

prize   trains   match   temperatures

b 🔊 8.5 Listen to the second part of the radio programmes and check.

> **STRATEGY** When you listen, think about the context of what you hear. How many people are speaking? Where are they? This can help you understand the topic.

Understanding the main idea

3 Listen to audio 8.5 again. Tick (✓) the best summary of what the people say.
1 a It's wet in Berlin and dry in Frankfurt. ☐
   b It's cold and icy everywhere in Germany. ☐
2 a Mandy is a famous writer. ☐
   b Mandy wants to take a short break from writing. ☐
3 a The tunnel from Switzerland to Italy is now open. ☐
   b The tunnel makes travelling between Switzerland and Italy very quick. ☐
4 a Both teams scored a goal in the first part of the match. ☐
   b The Dutch team won the match. ☐

WRITING Correcting mistakes

1 Read Katya's blog post about a news story. Find these numbers. What do they refer to?

a 22   _hours_
b 69   _____
c two   _____
d one billion _____
e 33   _____
f 31   _____

Last night I ⁽¹⁾**watch** the rescue of the Chilean miners on television. It was an amazing end to an amazing story. The 33 miners were under the ground for 69 days. It was very ⁽²⁾**comfortable** for them because the temperature was about 31 degrees and the tunnels were very wet.

Engineers working above the ground found the miners after about two weeks. They spoke to the miners every day with special video technology, and sent them food and water. They planned a way to get the miners out of the tunnels. The ⁽³⁾**miners** families stayed in tents near the mines and the Chilean president was often ⁽⁴⁾**their**, too.

So what happened next ⁽⁵⁾**!** The engineers rescued the first miner on 12 ⁽⁶⁾**october** 2010. It took 22 hours to rescue all of the miners. A lot of people from all over the world (about one billion!) watched the rescue on TV. It was incredible to see the miners and their families meet again!

2 Read the blog post again. Answer the questions.

1 How long were the miners under the ground?
   They were under the ground for 69 days.
   _____

2 How did the engineers speak to the miners?
   _____
   _____

3 What did the engineers send the miners?
   _____
   _____

4 Where did the miners' families stay?
   _____
   _____

5 When did the engineers rescue the first miner?
   _____
   _____

3 There are six mistakes in Katya's blog post. Look at the mistakes in **bold**, 1–6, and match them to Katya's notes, a–f.

1 grammar – tense   _b_
2 vocabulary   ____
3 punctuation   ____
4 spelling   ____
5 punctuation   ____
6 capital letters   ____

a This needs an apostrophe (') to show possession.
b This verb needs to be in the past simple.
c This is a month, so it needs a capital letter.
d I need to use a question mark (?) here.
e You spell this word 'there'.
f I need to use a word with the opposite meaning here.

4 Write a blog post about an interesting news story. When you finish, check your writing for mistakes.

> **TIP** Always check your writing for mistakes. If you find a mistake, think carefully about why it is wrong and try to correct it. If you can, swap your work with a partner. Find and underline any mistakes for him/her to correct.

9 Hungry planet

Vocabulary
Food & drink

1 a Find 12 food and drink words in the word snake. Which of these foods can you see in the picture?

gir**eggs**storangesphifruitjuicefelbreadrrahricepstomatoeschofishtlsyoghurtpotaolivessmcheesebeacarrotsglbbeans

b Which other foods can you see in the picture? _____

Talking about food

2 Complete the crossword with types of food and food verbs.

Across
2 I never … at home. I always eat out. (4)
3 When I'm too tired to cook I put a … pizza in the oven. (6)
4 My favourite food is a … in a bread roll with ketchup and chips. It's very unhealthy! (6)
5 I … a lot of fruit each day because it gives me energy. (3)
8 I never … food. I eat everything I buy. (5)
9 I … a cup of coffee on my way to work every morning. (3)

Down
1 I don't know much about food – the only thing I can … is a sandwich! (4)
2 I often buy … food because I can just cook it in the microwave. (11)
3 I buy … fruit and vegetables from the local market. (5)
6 I don't know why people … … old vegetables – I use them to make soup instead. (5, 4)
7 I ate a lot more … food, like burgers and pizzas, when I was younger. (4)

3 Rewrite the sentences in 2 so they are true for you.

Vocabulary extension
Food adjectives

4 a Label the pictures with the adjectives in the box.

creamy   delicious   disgusting   filling
healthy   ~~savoury~~   spicy   sweet

1 savoury

2 _____

3 _____

4 _____

5 _____

6 _____

7 _____

8 _____

b 9.1 Listen and check.

5 Circle the word in each list that you <u>can't</u> use with the adjective in **bold**.
1 **healthy:** apples, (chips,) tomatoes, fish
2 **savoury:** olives, pizza, sandwiches, sweets
3 **creamy:** yoghurt, lettuce, cheese, ice cream
4 **sweet:** cakes, pasta, biscuits, chocolate
5 **filling:** bread, potatoes, milk, rice

Bring it together

6 Choose the correct options to complete the letter.

Hi! I'm 25 and I study Law at university. I have exams soon and I'm very busy, so I don't have a lot of time to (1)(cook) / eat for myself. But I feel tired all the time and I think it's because of my diet. This is what I usually eat:

Breakfast: four (2)slices / sandwiches of white toast with butter; three (3)cups / glasses of coffee, with milk and two spoonfuls of (4)salt / sugar

Snack: something (5)sweet / savoury like a cake or a few biscuits

Lunch: pasta with cheese; two glasses of cola

Dinner: a frozen pizza or a (6)convenience / ready meal; three glasses of wine; a big (7)bowl / piece of ice cream

I want to be fit and healthy when I do my exams, but I don't know what to (8)make / buy when I go shopping. Please help me!
Elena Konidis

7 Complete the reply using the words in the box.

banana   bread   filling   fresh
healthy   juice   piece   ~~yoghurt~~

Dear Elena,
Thanks for your letter. I'm not surprised you feel tired all the time! If you want to be ready for your exams, try these ideas – I think you'll feel better very soon.

Breakfast
Have a bowl of cereal with a few spoonfuls of (1) _yoghurt_ . If you like, add some fruit – maybe a (2) _____ or an apple. To drink have black tea or a glass of fruit (3) _____ .

Snacks
It's OK to eat sweet things sometimes, but remember that these snacks aren't (4) _____ – you'll be hungry again soon! A (5) _____ of fruit is a good choice if you need energy.

Lunch
For lunch, try a soup or salad made with (6) _____ vegetables. If you're still hungry, have a slice of brown (7) _____ .

Dinner
At dinner, have some fish or chicken with rice and vegetables. Try not to eat too much convenience food – these meals are quick to make but they're not very (8) _____ !
Good luck!

9

GRAMMAR
Countable & uncountable nouns

1 Complete the table with the nouns in the box.

banana bread carrot fish milk
orange potato rice sugar water

Countable	Uncountable
banana	

2 Label the pictures with *a/an* or *some*.

1 *some* vegetables   2 _____ juice

3 _____ apple   4 _____ cakes

5 _____ tomato   6 _____ pasta

3 Choose the correct options to complete the descriptions of different breakfasts.

(1) *a* / *some* slice of toast and (2) *a* / *some* banana
(3) *a* / *some* fruit and (4) *a* / *some* bread with cheese
(5) *a* / *some* boiled egg and (6) *a* / *some* olives
(7) *a* / *some* rice and (8) *a* / *some* cup of coffee
(9) *a* / *some* bowl of soup with (10) *a* / *some* meat

4 Complete the article using *a/an* or *some*.

> Many meals from other countries seem difficult to make. However, sometimes the ingredients you need are already in your kitchen cupboard! Here are five examples:
>
> **Mehmet (Turkey)**
> My favourite food is hummus, which is very easy to make. All you need is some chickpeas (one tin), a lemon, some olive oil and (1) *some* salt!
>
> **José (Mexico)**
> Guacamole is very popular in Mexico, and doesn't take long to make. You need some avocados (at least two), a tomato, some chillis, (2) _____ onion (one large one) and (3) _____ lime juice.
>
> **Chairani (Indonesia)**
> To make chicken satay you need (4) _____ chicken (of course!) – about 500g is fine. You also need some peanut butter, some honey, some sesame oil, some garlic and (5) _____ spoonful of brown sugar. Simple!
>
> **Igor (Russia)**
> Borscht is a traditional soup from Russia, made with some beetroot (three or four small ones), some garlic, (6) _____ small potato, an onion and (7) _____ tomatoes.
>
> **Dominique (France)**
> Crêpes are great at any time of the day, and anyone can make them! You need (8) _____ butter (about 30g), (9) _____ egg, some flour, (10) _____ water and a small amount of milk (about 150ml).

5 Which dishes from your country use basic ingredients? Write a short description of a typical dish from your country.

56

Quantifiers

6 Write descriptions of the pictures. Use a quantifier from box A and a noun from box B.

A	B
a few	eggs
a lot of	fruit
not much	milk
too many	olives
too much	

1 *too much milk*   2 _____

3 _____   4 _____

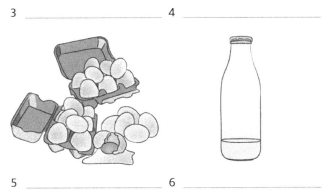

5 _____   6 _____

7 _____   8 _____

7 Complete the questions using *much* or *many*.

1 How *much* fast food do you eat?
2 How _____ cups of coffee do you have every day?
3 How _____ pasta or rice do you eat?
4 How _____ fresh fruit do you think we need to eat?
5 How _____ biscuits and cakes do you eat each week?

8 Choose the correct option to complete the sentences. Then match them to the questions in **7**.

a I don't eat much cake, but I have *a few* / *not many* biscuits every day.   5
b Quite a lot! I think I eat *too many* / *some* hamburgers and pizzas.   ___
c I don't eat much, but I eat *not many* / *a lot of* potatoes.   ___
d I think we need to eat *some* / *too much* every day.   ___
e Not *much* / *many*. Maybe two? I prefer tea.   ___

BRING IT TOGETHER

9 Complete the text with the words and phrases in the box.

a   an   how many   how much   a lot of
not many   some   ~~too much~~

When people think of McDonald's, they usually think of burgers and chips. But if you visit a McDonald's in another country, you might be surprised by the menu. We all know it's unhealthy to eat (1) *too much* fast food, so how about these alternatives? (2) _____ burgers like these have you tried?

India
In an Indian McDonald's, most of the food is made with vegetables. Many Indian people never eat meat, so (3) _____ burgers have meat in them. Why not try the 'McAloo Tikki', a spicy vegetable burger?

Taiwan
(4) _____ bread is in a Taiwanese 'Kao Fan' burger? The answer is none! Here they serve meat with small cakes made of rice. In Taiwan, you can eat your burger with (5) _____ chips or (6) _____ bowl of soup.

Argentina
In Argentina they eat (7) _____ beef but the 'McMila' sandwich only contains a very thin slice of beef! It is similar to an Argentinian dish called *milanesa*. For dessert, try (8) _____ ice-cream made with sweet *dulce de leche* sauce.

FUNCTIONAL LANGUAGE
Eating out

1 Put the words in the correct order to make sentences.

1 have can please we of red wine two glasses ?
   Can we have two glasses of red wine please?

2 for two we can please have a table ?
   _____

3 card by pay I can ?
   _____

4 have I please the antipasti can ?
   _____

5 you would the dessert menu to see like ?
   _____

6 I you can get to drink something ?
   _____

7 we the bill can have please ?
   _____

8 to order you are ready ?
   _____

9 like I'd please the tomato salad
   _____

10 please can the steak I have ?
   _____

2 a Complete the conversations with the sentences in 1.

A Hi, _2_
B Sure, here you are. ____
A Yes, ____ And a bottle of water.
B Certainly.

A ____
B Yes. To start with, ____
A Tomato salad, OK. And for you?
C ____
A That's fine. And for your main courses?
B Er, I'd like the lasagne, please.
C And ____ With chips.
A OK, coming right up.

A Can I take your plates?
B Yes, of course. Thank you.
A ____
C No, thank you. ____
A One moment, please. Here you are.
C Thank you. ____
A Yes, of course. That's no problem.

b 🔊 9.2 Listen and check.

LISTENING Predicting

1 a Look at the photos. Tick (✓) the foods you think you need to make *pasta napolitana*.

b 🔊 9.3 Listen to the first part of a cookery programme and check.

2 a Look at recipe steps a–f. Number them 1–6 in the order you think they go in.

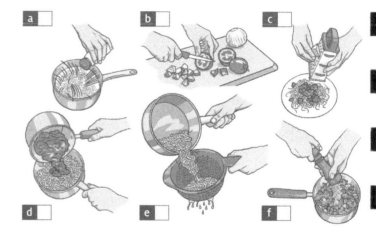

b 🔊 9.4 Listen to the second part of the cookery programme and check.

STRATEGY Before you listen, use what you know about the topic to predict information in the listening text. This can help you follow the text, even if you don't understand all the words.

Specific information

3 Listen to audio 9.4 again. Are the sentences true (T) or false (F)?

1 You need two small onions to make *pasta napolitana*. T /(F)
2 You cook the vegetables for five minutes. T / F
3 To cook the pasta, you need three litres of water. T / F
4 You cook the pasta for about eight minutes. T / F
5 The meal is ready in 20 minutes. T / F

READING Skimming

1 Read the article quickly and choose the best title.
1 Give waste food to supermarkets
2 Using waste to help the community
3 Supermarkets cook for the community

1 _____ What about food that the supermarket can't sell? The answer is that they throw this food away. Every year supermarkets in the UK waste millions of tons of food because they have too much in their shops.

2 _____ In 2008, he started the charity *FoodCycle*. He asked supermarkets to give the food they normally throw away to the charity. *FoodCycle* can use the food the supermarkets donate to make healthy, delicious meals. Many supermarkets around the UK now work with the charity.

3 _____ They work with centres for young children, the homeless and the elderly. The *FoodCycle* staff think it is important for people to eat well, even if they don't have a lot of money. They hope to teach people about good food and how it can help to make you happy and healthy!

4 _____ Most of the volunteers are young people from schools and universities. They work very hard to make *FoodCycle* a success. The charity also helps these people: it gives them new skills and helps them do something positive for people in their community.

To find out more about *FoodCycle* and the work they do, visit www.foodcycle.org.uk

Using the first sentence of paragraphs

2 Match the missing sentences, a–d, to paragraphs 1–4.
a Kelvin Cheung was worried about this problem.
b Do you ever think about what happens to the fresh food in supermarkets at the end of the day?
c *FoodCycle* makes thousands of meals every year.
d So who does all the cooking?

3 Read the article again. Answer the questions.
1 How much food do UK supermarkets throw away every year?
   Supermarkets throw away millions of tons of food every year.
2 What does *FoodCycle* do with the food?

3 Which groups of people does the charity help?

4 How does *FoodCycle* help its volunteers?

STRATEGY When you read a difficult text, it is useful to look at the first line of each paragraph. This usually has the main idea and will help you understand what the paragraph is about.

PROGRESS TEST 3

GRAMMAR & VOCABULARY
(25 points)

1 Complete the email using the past simple form of the verbs in brackets. *(12 points)*

Hi everyone!

I'm here in Philadelphia at last! I **(0)** _____ *had* _____ *(have)* a really bad journey! I **(1)** _____ *(leave)* home on Friday morning but the plane from Madrid to London was late so I **(2)** _____ *(miss)* my plane to Philadelphia. I **(3)** _____ *(wait)* for five hours for the next flight! The plane journey was OK though – I **(4)** _____ *(sit)* next to another student, but we **(5)** _____ *(be)* really tired so we **(6)** _____ *(not/speak)* much. I **(7)** _____ *(read)* my book for a while and then I **(8)** _____ *(go)* to sleep. In the end, we **(9)** _____ *(not/arrive)* in Philadelphia until 3 o'clock in the morning! The city **(10)** _____ *(be)* beautiful at that time. There **(11)** _____ *(not/be)* many people in the streets, but I **(12)** _____ *(see)* all the lights and skyscrapers in the centre!

Missing you lots! Love,

Jaime

2 Complete the questions. Answer them with short answers. *(4 points)*

0 When _did Jamie leave_ (leave) home?
  On Friday morning

1 Why _____ (miss) the plane to Philadelphia?
  _____

2 How long _____ (wait) for the next plane?
  _____

3 What time _____ (arrive) in Philadelphia?
  _____

4 _____ (be) a lot of people in the city centre?
  _____

3 Add three more words to each group. *(3 points)*

rainy _____ _____ | pasta _____ _____

weather | **food**

_____ _____ | _____ _____

bus _____

transport

_____ _____

4 Read the definitions and complete the words. *(6 points)*

0 You listen to singers and bands at this event.
  l i v e   c o n c e r t

1 You say this when someone does well in an exam.
  c _ _ _ _ _ _ _ _ _ _ _ _ _ s

2 Food that's quick and easy to make.
  c _ _ _ _ _ _ _ _ e _ _ _ _ _

3 News about famous people's private lives.
  c _ _ _ _ _ _ _ _ y g _ _ _ _ p

4 A sweet dish you eat at the end of a meal.
  d _ _ _ _ _ _ t

5 A place where visitors can get advice about a town.
  t _ _ _ _ _ _ t i _ _ _ _ _ _ _ _ _ _ n

6 Stories and information about your country.
  n _ _ _ _ _ _ _ l n _ _ s

READING *(25 points)*

1 Read the article and complete the form on page 61. *(9 points)*

Sri Lanka makes world's biggest cup of tea

9 October, 2010

A team of tea-makers in Colombo, the capital of Sri Lanka, made a new Guinness World Record today. They made 4,000 litres of tea – the biggest cup of tea in the world!

The tea-makers started at 3 a.m. because they needed five hours to make the tea. First they mixed 4,500 litres of water, 64 kilograms of tea, 875 kilograms of milk powder and 160 kilograms of sugar. Then they put all these ingredients in an enormous red cup. It was 3 metres high and 2.5 metres wide! The organisers said this huge cup was the same as about 32,000 normal cups of tea.

Later, the tea-makers decided to take the tea around Colombo. They gave it to the local people in small cups. Alison Ozanne, a representative from Guinness World Records, watched the event and gave the organisers their official prize. She agreed that this cup of tea was a new world record. American tea-makers set the last world record in Kansas City in September 2009, when they made 3,000 litres of tea.

TEST 3

Guinness World Records
Representative information sheet

Representative: _Alison Ozanne_
Record: _World's Biggest Cup of Tea_
New record set:
Day: (1)_____ Month: (2)_____ Year: _2010_
Location:
Country: (3)_____ City: (4)_____
New record measurement:
(5)_____ metres / litres / kilograms *(circle the correct option)*

Old record set:
Month: (6)_____ Year: (7)_____
Location:
Country: (8)_____ City: _Kansas City_
Old record measurement:
(9)_____ metres / litres / kilograms *(circle the correct option)*

Certify new record? ☑

2 Read the article on page 60 again. Answer the questions. *(16 points)*

1 What time did the tea-makers start?
_____

2 How long did they need to make the tea?
_____

3 How many litres of water did they use?
_____

4 How much sugar did they use?
_____

5 What did they put the tea in?
_____

6 How many normal cups of tea did they make in total?
_____

7 Who did they give the tea to?
_____

8 Who decided that it was a new record?
_____

LISTENING *(25 points)*

1 🔊 T3 Listen to five people talking about breakfasts. Match speakers 1–5 to the questions they answer. There are two extra questions. *(14 points)*

	speaker
1 Do you always eat breakfast?	_____
2 What's a typical breakfast in your country?	_____
3 What's your favourite breakfast?	_____
4 What did you have for breakfast this morning?	_____
5 How many cups of coffee do you drink in the morning?	_____
6 What time did you have breakfast this morning?	_____
7 Who do you eat breakfast with?	_____

2 Listen again and complete the sentences. *(11 points)*

1 Speaker 1 had olive oil and some (1)_____ on her toast. To drink, she had coffee and (2)_____ .

2 Speaker 2 is from (3)_____ . Two typical breakfast foods from his country are (4)_____ and (5)_____ .

3 Speaker 3 has breakfast with her (6)_____ . She says that breakfast is always (7)_____ .

4 Speaker 4 ate at (8)_____ in the morning. Then he went to the (9)_____ with his son.

5 Speaker 5 always has (10)_____ in the morning. She only eats breakfast at the (11)_____ .

WRITING *(25 points)*

1 Read a blog post about a festival. Number paragraphs a–d in the correct order, 1–4. *(4 points)*

a ☐ As well as tequila, there is a lot of special food for this celebration. Sweet bread and sweets called 'sugar skulls' are very typical. Chicken *mole* (chicken with chocolate and chilli sauce) is also very popular.

b ☐ The festival started hundreds of years ago. Mexico is famous for this festival but many other countries have a similar celebration.

c ☐ This is my favourite celebration of the year! People think it's the same as Halloween, but it's very different. It's a time to celebrate and be happy, so we have a big family party.

d ☐ The *Día de los Muertos* or 'Day of the Dead' is on 2 November. On this day we remember friends and family members who died. We buy presents for them — toys for children and alcohol (tequila) for adults.

2 Which paragraph, a–d, answers these questions? *(6 points)*

☐ What's your opinion of the festival?
☐ When does it take place?
☐ What do people do?
☐ When did the festival begin?
☐ What do people eat and drink?
☐ What's the name of the festival?

3 Write a blog post about a festival in your country. Answer the questions in 2. *(15 points)*

61

10 STATE OF THE ART

VOCABULARY
Technology

1 Look at the pictures. Complete the names of the gadgets.

1 fl _a_ tscr _e_ _e_ n TV

2 MP3 pl __ y __ r

3 s __ tn __ v

4 d __ g __ t __ l c __ m __ r __

5 c __ mp __ t __ r g __ m __   6 l __ pt __ p

2 Read the sentences. Choose a gadget from **1** for each person.

YVAN: I drive a lot with my job, and I'm always going to new places. I often get lost! _____satnav_____

AKIKO: I want to learn something new. I'm going to do a photography course. _____

JENNY: I love running – I go for a run on the beach every day. Sometimes it's a bit boring though. _____

KARIM: I need a present for my teenage son. He loves computers and hanging out at home with his friends. _____

WILL: I'm going to go travelling next year. I need to keep in touch with my friends and family. _____

HANNA: I love watching films on the big screen, but the cinema is too expensive! _____

3 Underline the incorrect adjective in each sentence. Write adjectives with the opposite meaning.
1. Look at my <u>old</u> MP3 player! My parents gave it to me for my birthday last week.   _new_
2. This kind of digital camera is very difficult to use. It doesn't have a lot of features. _____
3. Computer games are really cheap these days. _____
4. What's wrong with this internet connection? It's really fast today. _____
5. I can't see the screen on this laptop very well. It's too big. _____
6. This flatscreen TV is very heavy compared to our old TV. _____

4 Complete the puzzle with the computer words. What do the shaded letters spell?

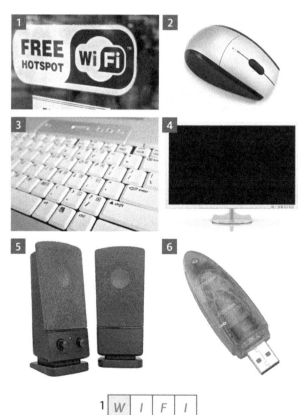

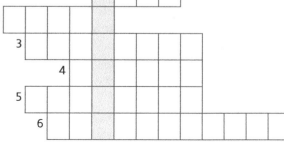

Communication verbs

5 Complete the phone messages with the words in the boxes.

call back   phone   ~~reply to~~

Hi Sylvain! Sorry I didn't (1) _reply to_ your email. I decided to (2) _____ you instead – I want to hear all about your holiday! But I guess you're out, so I'll (3) _____ later. Bye!

answer   ring   text

Hello? Priya? Please (4) _____ your phone! Where are you? Listen, we're going inside the theatre now. Can you (5) _____ me when you arrive? Don't (6) _____ me – you can't talk inside. OK, see you soon.

VOCABULARY EXTENSION
Technology verbs

6 Read the advice about using gadgets and technology. Do you do these things?

Technology top tips

Always **unplug** your gadgets when the battery is full. If you charge something for too long, it can be bad for the battery.

Be careful when you **download** things like music or video clips from the internet. Only use websites you know are safe.

Don't forget to **switch off** your gadgets when you're not using them. A laptop is small but it can waste a lot of energy!

It sounds simple, but make sure you **turn on** your gadget when you want to use it. This causes problems more often than you think!

7 a Match the verbs in **bold** in **6** to their opposites.

1 upload   _download_
2 turn off   _____
3 plug in   _____
4 switch on _____

b 🔊 10.1 Listen and check.

8 Complete the sentences with the words in the box.

~~download~~   plug in   switch on   turn off   upload

1 I often _download_ podcasts from the internet. Then I can listen to them on my MP3 player – it's more relaxing than music.
2 When I get to work in the morning, the first thing I do is _____ my computer.
3 I love this website. You can _____ photos to show them to your friends. See? This is me on holiday in Italy!
4 Is there somewhere I can _____ my laptop? I don't have any battery and I need to check my emails.
5 We're nearly home now, so you can _____ the satnav. We don't need it.

BRING IT TOGETHER

9 Read the reviews. Which gadget are they about?

a ☐   b ☐   c ☐

10 Complete the reviews with the words in the box.

download   easy   ~~expensive~~   keyboard   laptop
MP3 player   satnav   screen   text   Wi-Fi

It's here! The Maxi-smart is now in shops. At £249, this is an (1) _expensive_ gadget. Is it worth the money?
Tell us what you think…

The Maxi-smart is great! My favourite thing? The maps function. It works like a (2) _____ and it's brilliant when you're in a new place. You can use it to find a restaurant, café or car park nearby, too!

The (3) _____ on the Maxi-smart is really clear and bright – great for looking at photos or watching video clips. It is also good to have a REAL (4) _____, especially if you have big fingers like me! I think I'll (5) _____ more now, because it's much easier to write messages.

I don't like this phone. The battery life is very bad. You need to charge it every day! The (6) _____ function is OK – I use the internet when I'm on the bus or at college. But it's quite slow, especially if you want to (7) _____ music or anything. I prefer to use my (8) _____ for that.

I really like the Maxi-smart. The (9) _____ is great because I love listening to music. It's also very (10) _____ to use – I didn't need to read the instructions.

10

GRAMMAR
Comparative adjectives

1 Complete the crossword with the comparative form of the adjectives.

Across
3 fashionable (4, 11)
8 bad (5)
9 healthy (9)
11 safe (5)
12 big (6)
13 comfortable (4, 11)

Down
1 light (7)
2 expensive (4, 9)
4 fast (6)
5 happy (7)
6 difficult (4, 9)
7 good (6)
10 cheap (7)

2 Read the blog post. Six of the comparative adjectives in **bold** are incorrect. Find and correct the mistakes.

Today I got a new MP3 player. I love it because it's **smaller** and **more lighter** [*lighter*] than my old MP3 player, but it can store more songs. I can use it to store photos and video clips too. It's much **easyer** to use than my old MP3 player and the screen is **biger** and **brighter**. The best thing: it only cost €49! Of course, there are other models that are **expensiver**, but I don't think they are **gooder** than mine. Perhaps they look **more fashionabler**, but for me, features are **more important** than looks!

3 Complete the conversations with the comparative form of the adjectives in the box.

| ~~bad~~ | comfortable | difficult | fast |
| good | happy | relaxing | small |

1   A   Hey Sandra. How were your exams?
    B   Well, yesterday's exam was bad, but today's was even (1)_____*worse*_____! The questions were really hard – much (2)_____ than what we do in class.
    A   Oh no, poor you! At least your exams are all finished…
    B   Yeah, I'm a lot (3)_____ now!

2   A   What about this sofa? It looks (4)_____ than the one you have at the moment.
    B   Mm, I like it. But I need something (5)_____. That's too big for the flat.
    A   Oh, OK. Let's keep looking then.

3   A   I need to drive to Manchester tomorrow morning for work. The traffic's going to be terrible!
    B   Why don't you go by train? It's a lot (6)_____ than the car – it only takes an hour. The train's (7)_____, too. You can have a coffee, read the newspaper…
    A   You're right. That's a much (8)_____ idea. I'll go by train!

Going to

4 Look at Lisa's notes. Complete the sentences using the correct form of *going to*.

> tonight
> * go shopping
>   ~~- eggs~~
>   - vegetables
>   - rice
> * ~~coffee with Marie~~
> * call Omah about the party
>   (Rob and I can come!)

1 Lisa _____*is going to*_____ go shopping.
2 She _____ buy eggs.
3 Lisa and Marie _____ have coffee.
4 Lisa _____ call Omah.
5 Lisa and Rob _____ go to the party.

5 Put the words in the correct order to make sentences.

1 is go shopping tomorrow he going to
   He is going to go shopping tomorrow.

2 see Claire going to you are this weekend ?
   _____

3 I'm going to buy a new laptop not
   _____

4 going to Vicki to the cinema isn't come
   _____

5 phone are going to you later Paolo ?
   _____

6 this summer we're work going to in France
   _____

6 Complete the conversations using *going to* and the verbs in brackets.

1 A What are your New Year's resolutions? What
     (1) _____are_____ you __going to do__ (do)?
   B I (2) _____ (learn) Spanish! What about you?
   A Err, I (3) _____ (not make) any resolutions. I never keep them!

2 A What do you want to do tonight? Do you want to go out?
   B Sally (4) _____ (come) round for dinner. Don't you remember?
   A Oh yeah, of course! (5) _____ you _____ (cook)?

3 A (6) _____ you and Neil _____ (go) to Sziget again this year?
   B No, we're not. We (7) _____ (not buy) tickets for any music festivals. We need to save some money because we (8) _____ (travel) around Australia this summer.

Personal pronouns

7 Choose the correct options to complete the conversation.

A It's Ali's birthday next week, isn't it? What are you going to buy (1)*it / her / you*?

B I'm not sure. She gave (2)*me / I / her* a really good present for my birthday this year, so I want to get (3)*me / she / her* something special, too.

A Oh, really? What did she give (4)*him / you / her*?

B It was a CD that she made herself. With all my favourite songs on (5)*her / it / them*!

A What a great idea!

B I know. And two years ago my friends organised a weekend trip to the beach for (6)*they / me / them*. That was fun, too – it was really nice of (7)*them / they / us*.

A Wow! Did you go on your own then?

B Oh no, they came with (8)*I / them / me*! There were six of (9)*we / us / me*. We had a great time!

BRING IT TOGETHER

8 Complete the email using the words and phrases in the box. Change the form if necessary.

> cheaper   going to be   going to make
> going to meet   going to take
> going to upload   happier   ~~him~~   me   us

Hi everyone!
So you all know that Tom is in China at the moment but maybe you don't know that it's Tom's birthday next week. I want to organise a special surprise for (1) ___him___ . Can you help? It's very expensive to send presents and cards to China, so I have an idea that's much (2) _____ . I (3) _____ a birthday video for Tom. I (4) _____ the video to a website, so that he can watch it online.
I think Tom (5) _____ a bit sad on his birthday because he's a long way from his friends and family. But I think he'll be much (6) _____ when he sees all of (7) _____ singing 'happy birthday!'. We (8) _____ at my house on Thursday evening to record the video. It (9) _____ long to make the video – let (10) _____ know if you can make it!
Zara

FUNCTIONAL LANGUAGE
Giving instructions

1 a Match 1–5 to a–e to make phrases.

1 send — a the red button
2 click — b a name
3 key in — c 'video'
4 press — d on the menu
5 select — e a text message

b 🔊 10.2 Listen and check.

2 Complete the instructions about making a video using the phrases in **1**.

techpro231 says:

Here's how to record a video clip with your new phone...

1 First, (1) _click on the menu_ .
   You see some options.
2 Then (2) _____ .
   That starts the video camera.
3 Look at the screen. When you want to start recording, (3) _____ .
4 When you finish recording, (4) _____ for the video. Then you know which clip it is.
5 If you want to share the video with your friends, you can (5) _____ with the video clip.

Happy filming!

LISTENING Listening for gist

1 a 🔊 10.3 Listen to three conversations. Match each one to a gadget, a–c.

b Which conversation, 1–3, is about a problem with
  a a journey? ___ b an exam? ___ c technology? ___

Understanding informal English

2 a Listen to conversation 1 in audio 10.3 again. Match the words, 1–3, to the things they refer to.

1 this   a a button on the computer
2 them   b the webcam
3 that   c the people they want to talk to

b Listen to conversation 2 again. What do these words refer to?

1 it _____ 2 one _____ 3 there _____

3 Why do the speakers use the words in **2**? Choose the correct option.

1 They don't know the name of the things.
2 They know/can see what they are talking about so they don't need to repeat words.

4 a Look at transcript 10.3 on page 86. Listen to conversation 3 again. Cross out the words in the transcript that the speakers don't say.

b Are the statements true (T) or false (F)?

1 The boy is happy to talk about the exam.   T /(F)
2 He didn't study much for the exam.   T / F
3 He missed a lot of classes.   T / F
4 He didn't answer many questions.   T / F
5 He thinks he did well in the exam.   T / F

> **STRATEGY** Natural spoken English can be difficult to understand. Often people don't use complete sentences or don't explain what they mean. Listen to as much real-life English as possible. Try to identify in what ways it is different to formal English.

WRITING Planning

1 Read the email and answer the questions.

1 What is the relationship between Jamie and Isabel? _____

2 What does Isabel want to buy for Jamie? Why? _____

3 Why does she want a strong camera? _____

2 **a** <u>Underline</u> the questions in the email.

Hi Craig,
<u>How are you?</u> I'm writing to ask for advice. I know you love gadgets and Jamie wants a digital camera for his 18th birthday. The problem is, I don't know which one to buy. I looked at a lot of cameras last weekend. Some were smaller than others and some were more expensive. Is this important? Does a more expensive camera take better pictures? Also, you know my son likes dangerous sports. Are there any special, strong cameras? Please help – his birthday is next week!
Love, Isabel

b Read Craig's reply. Does it answer all Isabel's questions?

1 Hi Isabel, I'm fine thanks! Of course I can give you some advice about digital cameras.

2 First of all, cost is important. You usually get a better camera when you spend more money. You can get a good camera for about €200.

3 How big the camera is depends on what Jamie uses it for. Smaller cameras are better if you travel a lot because they're lighter. Sometimes bigger cameras take better pictures though.

4 Thinking about Jamie's hobbies, I suggest one of the new, strong digital cameras. Samsonic has a great one called Lumex. It can take pictures underwater!

Hope this helps! Craig x

3 Match Craig's notes, a–d, to paragraphs 1–4. Complete the notes.

    __4__ a *Strength: suggest the* ___Lumex___ *by Samsonic; takes photos* ___underwater___
    _____ b *Size: smaller = good for* _____; _____ *= better pictures*
    _____ c *Say hello, no problem giving advice*
    _____ d *Cost: important; more expensive =* _____ *camera*

4 Look at Robert's email. Write a reply giving him advice. Before you start, plan your reply. Use the notes in **3** to help you.

Hi, can you help me? I need to buy a computer, but I don't know which kind – a laptop or a PC? I work from home, but sometimes I go on business trips. Which do you think is better? Which is more expensive? Where can I look for good offers? Thanks!
Robert

TIP Before you start writing, make a plan. Write notes about what to include in each paragraph. This helps you remember everything and organise your work in a clear way.

11 A WORKING LIFE

VOCABULARY
Work & jobs

1 a Find 12 jobs in the word snake.

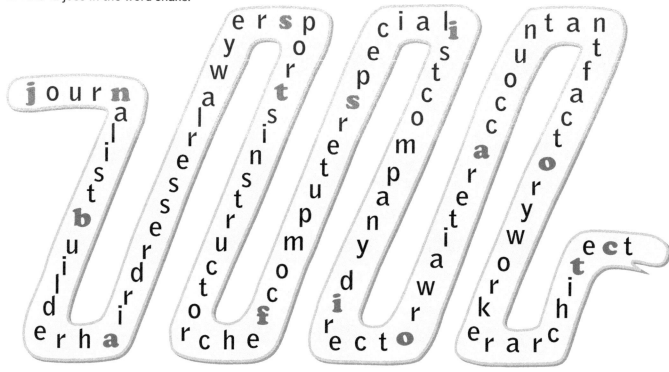

b Put the shaded letters in the correct order to make something people might want in their job.

| J | | | | | | | | | | | | | | | | | | | N |

2 Match the jobs in **1** to descriptions a–h.

a I work in a salon. I cut people's hair.
   hairdresser
b I teach people how to play tennis and football.
   _____
c I serve customers in a restaurant.
   _____
d I spend all day in a kitchen, cooking meals.
   _____
e I work in a big company. I make important decisions.
   _____
f I work in a huge building, using complicated machines to make new products.
   _____
g I can help you when you have a problem with your computer.
   _____
h I plan and design new buildings.
   _____

3 a Complete the sentences with adjectives.

1 I always feel good after a day in work. My job is really s _a_ _t_ _i_ _s_ _f_ _y_ _i_ _n_ g.
2 In my job I always have a lot to do. It can be very s _ _ _ _ _ _ _ l.
3 The best thing about my job is the high salary. It's very w _ _ _ _ _ _ d.
4 You need to be fit and healthy to do my job. It's really a _ _ _ _ e.
5 I don't make a lot of money from my job. It's quite b _ _ _ _ _ _ d.
6 It's important to stay safe in my job. Sometimes it can be very d _ _ _ _ _ _ _ _ s.
7 In my job I have to design and make things. It's very c _ _ _ _ _ _ e.
8 I love my job because every day is different. It's never b _ _ _ _ g.

b Which of the adjectives are a) positive? b) negative?

68

Work conditions

4 Complete the table with the words in the box.

~~contract~~ education part-time permanent
position qualifications retire
run (a business) salary skills temporary
training work (for yourself) unemployed

Adjectives	Verbs	Nouns
		contract

5 Complete the advertisement with words from **4**.

Do you love languages?
We might have the job for you!

We have a (1) ___position___ available for a friendly assistant to work in our London office. As part of the job, you will answer the telephone and talk to our colleagues all over Europe.

Job Details
- (2) _____ contract (four months only)
- (3) _____ , flexible hours (Monday, Tuesday and Thursday)
- good (4) _____ – £7 an hour
- language (5) _____ essential (French or Spanish)

You don't need a university (6) _____ or formal (7) _____ for this job, just a lot of energy and enthusiasm! Some experience is useful but don't worry – we give you full (8) _____ when you start work.

Interested?
See **www.lovelanguages.com** for more information.

BRING IT TOGETHER

6 Read the texts. The words in **bold** are incorrect. Write the correct words.

Q: I need job advice! What do you do? What do you like/not like about your job?

Ling22: I work for an international company as an (1)**accountant**. We design public buildings like schools and hospitals. The job is hard work, but it's really (2)**boring** – it's a great feeling when we finish a building! The days are very long though… I hope to (3)**work** my own business one day so I can decide my own working hours.

JakeW: I finished studying last year – I was (4)**employed** for eight months before I got a job! My new job is quite interesting but I'm worried because it's only a (5)**permanent** contract. What will I do in six months? More job applications??

Kez101: My job is really (6)**relaxing** – I'm always under a lot of pressure. That's difficult because in my job you can't get angry… EVER. The hours are terrible – sometimes I work all day and all night! And I'm not even (7)**badly** paid… Why do so many people want to do my job?? (I'm a junior doctor.)

GymGirl: I'm a sports (8)**teacher** at a local gym. I teach swimming, Pilates and yoga, things like that. I like my job because it's really (9)**creative** – I hardly ever sit down! It's a (10)**full-time** job so I only work a four-day week – that's good because I have two young kids.

1 ___architect___   6 _____
2 _____   7 _____
3 _____   8 _____
4 _____   9 _____
5 _____   10 _____

11

GRAMMAR
Superlative adjectives

1 Complete the sentences using the superlative form of the adjectives in brackets.
1 Some of _the richest_ (rich) people are computer specialists.
2 A doctor has one of _____ (responsible) jobs.
3 Accountants are some of _____ (well paid) workers.
4 Police officers have one of _____ (difficult) jobs.
5 Teachers have one of _____ (important) jobs.
6 Nurses are often _____ (friendly) people in a hospital.
7 An architect has one of _____ (creative) jobs.
8 Hairdressers are some of _____ (happy) workers.

2 Complete the sentences so they are true for you. Use the superlative form of the adjectives in brackets.
1 _Last year_ was _the happiest_ (happy) year of my life.
2 _____ is _____ (interesting) person I know.
3 _____ is _____ (big) city in my country.
4 _____ is _____ (good) time to visit my country.
5 _____ is _____ (expensive) thing I own.
6 _____ is _____ (young) person in my family.

Will/Won't

3 Complete the conversation using 'll, will or won't.
A Hi Danka, how are you?
B Great, thanks! I'm happy it's Friday. I'm going on holiday tomorrow! We're going to spend a week in Turkey.
A Sounds lovely! But wait, that means you (1) _won't_ be at the staff party next week.
B No, I (2) _____ . It's a real shame. Café Paradiso is such a good restaurant – I'm sure the food (3) _____ be delicious!
A Yeah, I hope so. When (4) _____ you be back in the office?
B I (5) _____ be back on the 15th.
I (6) _____ see you then!
A OK. Have a great holiday!

4 a Complete the questions about Bertil using will and a verb from the box.

| earn | meet | start | wear | ~~work~~ |

1 _Will_ he _work_ in an office?
  Yes, he will.
2 _____ he _____ work early?
3 _____ he _____ a uniform?
4 _____ he _____ nice people?
5 _____ he _____ a good salary?

b Read Bertil's message. Answer the questions using short answers.

Hey Emma,
I did it – I got the job! Monday will be my first day in the office – 11 a.m. to 7 p.m. It's great because the company is quite relaxed – I can wear what I want to work and the people are really friendly. The salary is good, too – let's go out when I get my first month's pay!
See you soon,
Bertil

11

Will & might

5 a Circle the correct option to complete what the people say.

Angie: This is my third year in this job, and I feel like I need a change. I (1) *won't / might* start looking for a new job soon, but I'm worried that it (2) *'ll / won't* take a long time because the economy isn't very strong at the moment.

Samir: I'm going to start a new job next week – I'm excited but a bit nervous, too. I (5) *might / won't* know any of the other people, so I keep asking myself: '(6) *Will / Might* I get on with them?' I hope they're nice!

Tomoko: Next year (3) *will / might* definitely be an important year for me. I'm going to finish my university degree and I need to decide what to do next. It (4) *might / might not* be easy to get a job – a lot of my friends had problems finding work.

Geoff: The company had a good year this year, so we (7) *might / might not* get a bonus – if we're lucky! But if we do, I (8) *'ll / won't* spend it on something expensive like a holiday – I think it's more important to save it for the future.

b 🔊 11.1 Listen and check your answers.

6 a Match 1–6 to a–f to make sentences.

1 Julia's new job is 200km away, so she
2 Tino failed his medical exams, so he
3 Simon got a pay rise last week, so he
4 Vinny applied for a new job last week so he
5 Handa has a business trip to Germany soon, so she
6 Erika has quite a lot of work to do today, so she

a _____ have an interview soon.
b _____ need to book a flight and hotel room.
c _____ become a doctor.
d _____ go home until very late.
e *will* need to move house.
f _____ get more money this month.

b Complete the sentences using *'ll, will, won't, might* or *might not*.

BRING IT TOGETHER

7 a Read the conversation. What job is Kris applying for?

A Hello Kris, nice to meet you.
B Nice to meet you too, Mr White.
A So, Kris, why do you want to work here at The Kitchen?
B I really love cooking! If you give me a job, I (1) *'ll* work really hard. And I'm very organised. I (2) _____ be late for work!
A In this job, you need to work some evenings and weekends. Some people (3) _____ like that. What do you think?
B That's no problem. A job with flexible hours is perfect for me.
A OK. It can be very busy here, so you (4) _____ find the job stressful at times. (5) _____ that be a problem?
B No, it (6) _____ . I like being busy!
A That's good to know. Well thank you for coming, Kris.
B Thank you, Mr White. When (7) _____ I hear about the job?
A I (8) _____ call you on Monday.
B OK, thank you very much.

b Complete the conversation using *'ll, will, won't, might* or *might not*.

8 Read what two people say about Kris's interview. Complete the conversation using the superlative form of the adjectives in the box.

creative   ~~friendly~~   good   important   young

A I thought Kris was very nice – she was definitely (1) *the friendliest* person.
B That's true. But she was also (2) _____ candidate. Does she have any experience? That's (3) _____ thing for this job.
A Not much. But she has a lot of ideas. I think she was (4) _____ person.
B OK, I think you're right. Kris was (5) _____ candidate. Let's give her the job!

FUNCTIONAL LANGUAGE
Offers & requests

1 a Match 1–6 to a–f to make sentences.

1 Can you
2 Let me
3 I'll get
4 Can you help
5 Will you close
6 I'll call

a me with the cooking?
b you this evening!
c answer the phone for me?
d the window, please?
e that for you.
f buy you a coffee.

b 🔊 11.2 Listen and check your answers.

2 Match sentences 1–6 in **1** to pictures g–l.

LISTENING
Understanding the main idea

1 🔊 11.3 Listen to two people talking about jobs. Choose the correct option to complete the sentences.

1 Anna needs to earn money to go to university / Paris.
2 Anna's job is more *interesting / boring* than Tim's job.
3 Tim liked *everything / some things* about his job.
4 Tim is Anna's *friend / brother*.

Key information

2 Look at the words and phrases in the box. Match them to Anna's job, Tim's job or neither.

> boring   cleaning   easy   long hours
> museum   part-time   satisfying   well paid

Anna's job	Tim's job	Neither
boring		

3 a Complete the sentences with words from **2**.

1 Anna is doing _____ to earn money.
2 She works _____ hours.
3 She thinks the job is _____ .
4 Tim worked in a _____ .
5 His job was _____ .
6 In his job, he worked _____ .

b Listen again and check your answers.

4 Look at transcript 11.3 on page 86. Listen to the conversation again and underline the words which are stressed (spoken more loudly or clearly than other words).

> **STRATEGY** As you listen, remember to listen for key information words. Usually, the key words are stressed, because they are important.

READING Supporting ideas

1 Read the article about Kevin Richardson. Are sentences 1–4 true (T) or false (F)?

a Kevin Richardson has an unusual job. He works with lions and other big cats at an animal park in South Africa. [1] Kevin often spends all day with these dangerous animals. [2] He stays with them 24 hours a day, training them so they become his friends. He regularly swims and evens sleeps with the lions.

b [3] Kevin loved animals from a very early age. [4] _____ Kevin spent a lot of time with the birds. When he watched them, he noticed that each bird had a different personality. He needed to treat them all differently if he wanted to have a good relationship with all of them.

c Kevin knows that his job is dangerous. [5] Recently, one of his lions attacked him, but luckily, the attack was not serious. [6] _____ Kevin thinks he was responsible for the attack because he made the lion angry. He doesn't worry about the dangers of his work because he thinks he has the best job in the world.

d Kevin now uses his skills to make films and television programmes. A few years ago, the famous film-maker Michael Rosenberg visited the animal park in Johannesburg. He saw Kevin playing with the lions and decided to make a programme about this special relationship. [7] The programme was very popular so Kevin made more films about the different animals in South Africa. [8] _____

1 Kevin has a good relationship with the animals at the park.	(T)/ F
2 He believes all animals are the same.	T / F
3 Kevin doesn't think his job is dangerous.	T / F
4 Not many people know about Kevin's work.	T / F

2 **a** Look at the underlined words in sentence 1 in the text. In sentence 2 find

1 a word that refers to 'Kevin'   _He_

2 a word that refers to 'these dangerous animals'   _____

3 a phrase that means 'all day'   _____

b Read sentences 3, 5 and 7 in the text again and underline the key words and phrases. Choose the best sentence, a or b, to complete gaps 4, 6 and 8.

Gap 4

a He often went to hospital when he was young because the animals attacked him. ☐

b When he was young, his parents gave him a parrot, snakes, mice and birds to look after. ☐

Gap 6

a The lion injured Kevin's arm but then it stopped attacking him. ☐

b Kevin nearly died because the lion hurt him so badly. ☐

Gap 8

a He hopes the films will teach people about these beautiful and interesting animals. ☐

b He thinks the films will make people want to come to his country as tourists. ☐

STRATEGY Each sentence in a paragraph usually contains words and phrases which refer to or support the main idea of the paragraph. If you find a sentence hard to understand, look at the sentences before and after it to help you.

12 LISTMANIA!

■ VOCABULARY
Dreams & ambitions

1 Complete the ambitions using the verbs in box.

be   do   ~~go~~   have   make   run

1 _____go_____ on a round-the-world trip
2 _____ my own boss
3 _____ a parachute jump
4 _____ a fortune
5 _____ a marathon
6 _____ a big family

2 Complete the sentences with the ambitions in **1**.

1 I've always been very unfit. Recently, I decided to do something about it and I started exercising more. Now I want to _run a marathon_ – but I still have a lot of training to do!

2 After 15 years, I'm bored with my job. I really want to start my own company. I'd like to _____ at last!

3 Money – that's all I want! If I have to work really hard, that's fine. I just want to get rich – my dream is to _____ !

4 I'd love to do something really exciting or dangerous – even just for a few minutes. Next year, I plan to _____ – I think it'll be amazing!

5 After school, all my friends had a year off, but I went straight to university. When I finish studying, I want to go travelling – maybe I'll even _____ !

6 I'm an only child, and I always wanted a brother or sister. That's why I'd love to _____ . I don't want my son to feel the same way I did.

Common verbs & collocations

3 Complete the sentences with the phrases in the box.

children   a great job   a good time   any housework
a message   notes   a phone call   a rest
some shopping   ~~a shower~~

1 I'll be ready to go out in about half an hour. I just need to have __a shower__ .
2 Thanks for coming to the party last night. I hope you had _____ .
3 Sally's not in the office at the moment. Can I take _____ ?
4 You look exhausted, Theo. You need _____ .
5 Anja isn't interested in a career. All she wants to do is get married and have _____ .
6 Can you turn your music down, please? I need to make _____ .
7 My flatmate is really lazy. I can't remember the last time she did _____ .
8 I might be a bit late home tonight. I need to do _____ after work.
9 Sorry I missed the meeting this morning. Did you take _____ for me?
10 We were happy with the people that painted our flat. They did _____ .

4 ◀))) 12.1 Listen to five conversations. Number the phrases 1–5 in the order you hear them.

lunch _____   some cooking _____   a holiday _____
a list _____   a taxi __1__

5 a Choose the correct word to complete the extracts.

1 It's not far – about a twenty-minute walk. But the best thing to do is to *make / (take)* a taxi from the station.
2 I'm afraid Mrs Sanderson is out of the office at the moment. She's *having / taking* lunch with some clients.
3 I didn't know whether to leave my last job. So, I sat down and *made / did* a list of all the good and bad things about it.
4 To be honest, I feel like *doing / making* some cooking. Something really nice for a change.
5 I'm not sure. He and Mum want to *have / do* a holiday. Then they'll see what happens when they get home.

b Listen again and check.

74

Describing places

6 Match 1–6 to a–f to make phrases.

1	state-of-the-art	a	culture
2	fresh	b	lakes
3	relaxed	c	hotels
4	cosmopolitan	d	airport
5	top quality	e	atmosphere
6	wonderful	f	air

7 Complete the sentences with the phrases in **6**.

1 We're really lucky because there are two
_____wonderful lakes_____ near the city. In summer, we go
swimming every weekend!

2 When I go away, I don't stay in _____ .
Hostels are better if you want to see what a city is really
like.

3 I love the _____ here. You can meet
people from all over the world.

4 You can fly anywhere in the world from the city's
_____ .

5 We went walking in the mountains yesterday. It was so
nice to be out in the _____ !

6 There's a very _____ here. The people
are really friendly and welcoming.

8 Complete the description of a city using the words in
the box.

architecture   cost of living   cultural life
green hills   ~~job opportunities~~   location
tourist attractions   transport system

'I came to the city for the **(1)** _job opportunities_
it's a lot easier to find work here. But the
(2) _____ is fantastic – there are
cinemas, theatres and museums everywhere! The
(3) _____ is interesting, too – I love the
mix of old and new buildings. I think it's a good place
for visitors because there are a lot of things to see
and do. Some of the **(4)** _____ are quite
expensive, though. That's the worst thing about the
city – the **(5)** _____ is quite high. Flats
are really expensive and it costs a lot of money to
use the bus or the tram. The **(6)** _____
is good though – it's really easy to travel anywhere.
In half an hour, you can be in the country, with
(7) _____ and mountains all around.
I think the **(8)** _____ is one of the best
things about the city – it's in such a beautiful, natural
setting.'

BRING IT TOGETHER

9 Complete the texts with the words in the box.

atmosphere   cosmopolitan   a good time   have
~~holiday~~   location   take   tourist attractions

I moved to the city a few weeks ago. This weekend
my friends are going to visit me because they want to
have a short **(1)** _holiday_ . I'd like them to
have **(2)** _____ while they're here! The only
problem is I don't have a lot of money at the moment.
All the **(3)** _____ are quite expensive – if
we go to the museum or the art gallery in the day, we'll
need somewhere cheap to eat in the evening. Does
anybody have any suggestions??

| Tags | restaurants | cheap | comments (2) |

comments

Hi NLK,
Take your friends to the Old Quarter – it's a really great
place to **(4)** _____ dinner. The area is very
(5) _____ and you can eat food from all over
the world: Indian, Thai, Italian, Mexican, Turkish...
(Café Coco is good!) It's my favourite part of the city –
the **(6)** _____ is amazing, really relaxed.
To get there, **(7)** _____ the bus from
Alexander Square (number 12 or 33) and get off at
James Street. Have fun! 😊

I went to Café Coco with my friends last Saturday – great
restaurant in a great **(8)** _____ ! Thanks JoJo!

75

12

GRAMMAR
Present perfect: *Have you ever...?*

1 a Complete the questions using the past participles of the verbs in brackets.

Have you ever...
1 _done_ (do) a dangerous job?
2 _____ (fly) a hot-air balloon?
3 _____ (visit) an English-speaking country?
4 _____ (go) skiing?
5 _____ (read) a book in another language?
6 _____ (see) an elephant?
7 _____ (win) a race?
8 _____ (work) in a big city?

b Match questions 1–8 to pictures a–h.

a 8 b ___ c ___ d ___
e ___ f ___ g ___ h ___

2 Complete the sentences using short answers. Match them to five of the questions in **1**.

a Yes, _I have_ ! I went to the USA last summer.   3
b No, _____ . I work in an office so it's pretty safe! ___
c Yes, _____ . When I was younger I had a job in Milan. ___
d Yes, _____ – I ran a lot when I was at school and I won the 100 metres race one year! ___
e No, _____ , but I sometimes read articles from English newspapers. ___

Present perfect & past simple

3 Choose the correct option to complete the sentences.
1 *Have you ever run* / *Did you ever run* a marathon?
2 *Have you been* / *Did you go* to London at the weekend?
3 He *has been* / *went* to India last summer.
4 *Have you met* / *Did you meet* my friend Carla?
5 I *have never been* / *never went* horse-riding.

4 Complete the conversations with the correct form of the verbs in brackets.

1 A (1) _Have_ you ever _been_ (go) to Brazil, Nick?
   B No, I haven't. I (2) _____ (visit) Argentina last year but I (3) _____ never _____ (go) to Brazil. What about you?
   A Well, my mum's Brazilian, so I (4) _____ (live) there when I was young. In São Paulo.
   B Really? I didn't know that!

2 A Hi Zsofi, you look great! (5) _____ you _____ (go) to your yoga class this morning?
   B Yeah, I did – it was so relaxing! (6) _____ you ever _____ (do) yoga?
   A Yes, once. I (7) _____ (have) a yoga lesson when I was on holiday last year.
   B (8) _____ you _____ (like) it?
   A Not really. I prefer going for a run!

76

Review of verbs

5 Complete the blog post with the correct form of the verbs in brackets.

My new flat?

My name's Deeny and I **(1)** _live_ (live) in Singapore with my husband and my parents. At the moment, we **(2)** _____ (look) for a flat of our own. All the flats in the city centre are very expensive: we **(3)** _____ (can) afford to live there. But last week we **(4)** _____ (visit) five flats outside the city. One of them **(5)** _____ (be) great, we really liked it! It's about half an hour from the city centre but the transport connections are very good. If we move there, it **(6)** _____ (be) difficult to travel to work. Tomorrow we **(7)** _____ (see) the flat for the second time. I hope we move soon – I **(8)** _____ (be) really happy when we have our own place!

BRING IT TOGETHER

6 Read the article about Ali and Lorna. Complete the article using phrases a–h.

a will be great to go for a walk
b will have safer and healthier lifestyles
c are now doing the same thing
d can enjoy the peace
e am getting old
f moved to London when he was 18
g are going to sell
h has never lived in the country

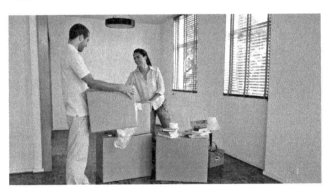

Selling their house in the city and moving to the country is something people often do after they retire. However, many younger people **(1)** _c_ . They enjoy city life, but they want to move to a place where they **(2)** _____ . One young couple, Lorna McDonald and Ali Hameed, **(3)** _____ their small flat in London and buy a bigger house in a village 25 km away. Ali, a teacher, was born in the country but **(4)** _____ because he thought life in his village was boring. He loves London – the bars, restaurants and cinemas – but he will be happy to escape from the traffic and pollution of the capital. 'It **(5)** _____ through the village. We **(6)** _____ , the clean air, and the green spaces,' he said. Lorna **(7)** _____ but she thinks she will enjoy the peace and quiet. 'Maybe I **(8)** _____ ,' she said, 'but I don't think I'll miss the nightlife. I like going to bed early now!'

7 a Who said the sentences, Ali (A) or Lorna (L)?

1. When I was younger, I always went to bed late, but now I like an early night!

2. I hated living in a small place when I was a teenager.

3. I can live in the country and still work at a school in the city.

b 12.2 Listen and check.

FUNCTIONAL LANGUAGE
Finding out & recommending

1 Put the words in the correct order.

a like it what's ?
   What's it like?

b you recommend where do ?
   _____

c amazing everyone the food says is
   _____

d eaten ever there you have ?
   _____

e love you'll it !
   _____

f to a good you place eat recommend can ?
   _____

2 a Complete the conversation with phrases a–f from **1**.

1 A So Gianni, (1) _f_ ?
     I'll book a table for tonight.
  B Good idea! There's a great Turkish restaurant about five minutes away. It's really popular.
  A That sounds great. (2)_____ ?
  B No, I haven't, but (3)_____.
     I'd like to try it!

2 A Excuse me, can you help us? We're looking for somewhere to have a drink near here.
  B Well, you're in the right place! This area is famous for its nightlife.
  A Really? That's good. (4)_____ ?
  B Well, my favourite bar is The Lounge. It's just round the corner.
  A Sounds good! (5)_____ ?
  B Relaxed atmosphere, great music...
     (6)_____ !

b 🔊 12.3 Listen and check.

LISTENING
Listening for gist

1 🔊 12.4 Listen to a radio programme about Mark Beaumont. Choose the correct answer a, b or c.

1 Mark Beaumont is famous for
  a cycling   b running   c exploring.

2 Before going around the world, Mark travelled in
  a Italy and Argentina
  b Italy and the UK
  c Argentina and the USA.

3 In the future, Mark plans to
  a stop cycling
  b travel around the UK
  c go on another trip.

Using questions

2 a Look at the questions. <u>Underline</u> the key words.
  1 <u>Where</u> did <u>Mark</u> <u>live</u> when he was <u>young</u>?
    _____
  2 How long did Mark's journey around the world take?
    _____
  3 What two things helped him complete the trip?
    _____
  4 What problems did Mark have in the Americas?
    _____
  5 What other activity did Mark do in the Americas?
    _____

b What can you remember? Make notes about the questions.

3 Listen again and check your answers in **2**.

> **STRATEGY** Before you listen, read the questions carefully and underline the key words. This can help you find the answers in the listening.

WRITING Organising your ideas

1 Read the book review. Is it positive or negative? _____

HelenaB *29/11/10*

Last month, I read *Yes Man* by Danny Wallace. I think you'll love this book! I'm going to buy it for all my friends and I'm going to say 'yes' more! Danny is the main character of this book. At the start of the book, his life is quite boring. He hardly ever sees his friends because he prefers to stay at home. This book is funny and interesting. It changed the way I think about my life. One day, a strange man tells Danny to 'say yes more'. So for one year, Danny says 'yes' to every question and invitation – he has some very interesting experiences!

2 a Read the review again. What is the problem with the writing?
1 The verbs are often in the wrong tense. ☐
2 The sentences are in the wrong order. ☐
3 The sentences are too long. ☐

b Rewrite the review using the writing plan.

1 Introduction: the name of the book and the writer
2 Information about the character(s) and the story
3 What the reviewer thought about the book
4 What other readers will think about the book

3 a Think of a book you read recently. Complete the notes.

THE NAME OF THE BOOK   _____
THE WRITER OF THE BOOK   _____
THE MAIN CHARACTER(S)   _____
YOUR RATING   ☆ ☆ ☆ ☆ ☆

b Write a review of the book. Use your notes and the plan in **2b** to help you.

TIP Before you start writing, think carefully about how to organise your ideas. What will you write about first? How will you end your piece of writing? Make notes to help you.

PROGRESS TEST 4

GRAMMAR & VOCABULARY
(25 points)

1 Complete the second sentence so it means the same as the first. Use the word in **bold** and one other word. *(12 points)*

0 This is the first time I've used an e-reader. **(never)**
   I've _never_ _used_ an e-reader before.

1 Digital cameras are now cheaper than Polaroid cameras. **(expensive)**
   Polaroid cameras are now _____ _____ than digital cameras.

2 It's possible that in 20 years, we will use e-readers, not books. **(might)**
   In 20 years, we _____ _____ e-readers, not books.

3 You can't buy a laptop lighter than this one. **(the)**
   This is _____ _____ laptop you can buy.

4 What are your plans for this weekend? **(to)**
   What are you _____ _____ do this weekend?

5 I went to Santiago in 2008 and in 2010. **(been)**
   I _____ _____ to Santiago twice.

6 I'll help you with those books. **(let)**
   _____ _____ help you with those books.

2 Circle the word in each list that you <u>can't</u> use with the verb in **bold**. *(5 points)*

0	**run**	a business	a marathon	(a job)
1	**work**	from home	good pay	long hours
2	**send**	an email	a text message	a phone call
3	**make**	a salary	a fortune	a living
4	**have**	a good time	a mistake	children
5	**take**	a list	the bus	a message

3 Complete the sentences with words from the box. There are four extra words. *(8 points)*

> atmosphere attractions banker cheap
> contract culture opportunities slow
> TV waiter webcam work

1 I don't like sending text messages, it's very _____ .
2 Buenos Aires is famous for its cosmopolitan _____ .
3 This is a great city to live in but there aren't many job _____ .
4 Shireen bought a new flatscreen _____ last week.
5 Everyone at work is friendly and there's a very relaxed _____ .
6 My boyfriend is a _____ . He works in an office in the city centre.
7 I always talk to my sister online – it's great because we can use the _____ .
8 The job is only temporary – it's a six-month _____ .

READING *(25 points)*

1 Read the interview. Complete the interview with questions a–f. *(12 points)*

a What's the worst job you've ever done?
b What advice are you going to give our readers today?
c How will work change in the future?
d What was your first job?
e Do you like this job?
f How many jobs have you had?

At *Work World* our careers advisors will help you find your dream job. But what qualifications do you need to be a careers advisor? Michael Weissman, one of our top advisors, tells us about his experience.

Hi Michael. Thanks for talking to us today.

You're welcome, I'm happy to be here.

(1) _____ ?

Oh, it was a part-time job in a supermarket. I was 16. When I was 18 I used the money I earned to buy a motorbike!

(2) _____ ?

I can't remember! I've worked as an office worker, a waiter and a journalist. I also worked in a factory one year. The office job was the most boring position!

(3) _____ ?

I cleaned windows one winter. It was very hard work, very physical. And the weather was awful – freezing and windy. I earned quite a lot of money, but I still hated that job!

(4) _____ ?

Yes, I love it. I like writing for *Work World*, but the best thing about the job is working with people. It's really satisfying when we help someone to change or improve their career – there are so many people who want a better job.

(5) _____ ?

If you love your work, it's not work. Don't do a job for the money, you'll never be happy. Do it because it's interesting.

(6) _____ ?

People say that in 20 years, we will all work from home. I think people will still prefer to travel to work because they like working in a team more than working alone. One thing I can say is that we will definitely use computers for nearly every job!

80

TEST 4

2 Choose the correct options to complete the summary of the interview. *(13 points)*

Michael Weissman is a ⁽¹⁾ *careers / qualifications* advisor. He started working when he was ⁽²⁾ *16 / 18*. For his first job, he worked as a ⁽³⁾ *shop assistant / waiter*. He ⁽⁴⁾ *does / doesn't* know how many jobs he has done but he says the most ⁽⁵⁾ *interesting / boring* job was working in an office. Michael ⁽⁶⁾ *liked / didn't like* his window cleaning job because of the ⁽⁷⁾ *weather / salary*. Michael's favourite thing about his job as a careers advisor is ⁽⁸⁾ *writing / working* with people. He says that ⁽⁹⁾ *a lot of / not many* people want to change their job. Michael thinks it's important to do a job that is ⁽¹⁰⁾ *well paid / interesting* if you want to be happy. He thinks that, in 20 years, people ⁽¹¹⁾ *will / won't* want to work from home because they ⁽¹²⁾ *like / don't like* working in a team. Michael is ⁽¹³⁾ *sure / not sure* that, in the future, computers will be important for nearly all jobs.

LISTENING *(25 points)*

1))) T4 Listen to the TV show and complete the table. *(9 points)*

	Question 1 (favourite gadget?)	Question 2 (how many countries?)	Question 3 (favourite place?)	Question 4 (summer plans?)
Jim said...	iPod			Ireland, visit cousins
Maggie said...				
✓/✗	✓			

2 Listen again and answer the questions. *(16 points)*

1 Where are Jim and Maggie from?

2 How long have they been married?

3 Does Jim work?

4 What is Maggie's job?

5 What countries does Maggie say she has visited?

6 Why is Paris her favourite place?

7 What is Maggie going to do in New York?

8 Do Jim and Maggie win?

WRITING *(25 points)*

1 Read Suresh's blog post. What two problems does he have? *(2 points)*

www.englishforum.co.uk

The best place for English students worldwide

Suresh says:

Hi,

My second year of English classes isn't going very well. Last year I learned a lot of new words, but now I can't remember them! The worst thing is that I speak really slowly because I don't want to make mistakes. I don't know what to do! Can you help?

2 January 2011, 8:45 AM

Patricia says:

Hi Suresh,

I study English, too – I started an English course last year. Here's my advice for you. Has you ever made a vocabulary list? Every day I write new words in a notebook and I look at them when I'm on the bus to work. I can to remember them this way!

Don't worry about doing mistakes when you speak – everybody says the wrong things sometimes! The more important thing you can do is practise. If you often speak in English, you won't speak more quickly! Every week, I take lunch with an American friend. We talk in English, then in Spanish, so it's good for both of we! My English is a lot gooder now. Good luck!

Patricia

2 January 2011, 4:22 PM

Post a comment

2 Read Patricia's reply to Suresh. Find and correct eight mistakes. *(8 points)*

3 How do you learn new vocabulary and practise speaking? Write a reply to Suresh, giving him your advice. *(15 points)*

TRANSCRIPTS

to a box in the corner of the pool. A different player comes into the game. Men and women can play this sport and sometimes there are men and women in the same team. If you want to know more about underwater rugby, visit www.underwatersports...

6.1, p. 35, Ex 7

Clothes: outfit, spotty, denim, sandals, handbag
Face: freckles
Hair: curly, ponytail

6.2, p. 38, Ex 2

1 A: Hello, can I help you?
   B: Oh, no thanks. I'm just looking.
2 A: I'm looking for a pair of black boots.
   B: OK. What size do you need?
3 A: Where are the changing rooms, please?
   B: They're at the back of the shop, next to the shoe department.
4 A: Excuse me, how much are these?
   B: They're 52 Euros. Do you want to try them on?
5 A: Do you have this in a bigger size?
   B: No, sorry. That's the only size we have.
6 A: Can I pay by card?
   B: Sorry, no. We only take cash.
7 A: Can I try this on?
   B: Yes, of course. The changing rooms are over there.
8 A: Do you have these in other colours?
   B: Yes, we do. We have dark blue, red and black.

6.3, p. 38, Exs 1–3

1 A: Hello, welcome to Foxton Electronics. Can I help you?
   B: Err, yes please. I'm looking for a new television.
   A: Well sir, we have an incredible sale on today. Our top model is usually £999, but today it costs just £949. And, we give you a free DVD player!
   B: Oh, OK. That's still quite expensive...
   A: But just look at it, the V430... The picture is fantastic!
   B: Uh, well, yeah, it's nice. It's very big though.
   A: But sir, you just can't miss out on this offer!
   B: Well, I don't know. Can I think about it? Maybe I'll come back tomorrow.
2 A: See you later! Love you!
   B: Oh, where are you going?
   A: I'm meeting Tom for a coffee.
   B: Oh, really? Again? Uh, why don't I come with you?
   A: Well, we need to talk about work – Tom's helping us with a project at the moment. It'll probably be really boring.

B: Hey, don't worry. I want to know more about what you're doing... I just need to get my jacket.
A: Right, OK.

3 A: Good morning Mr Rodriguez. Can I talk to you for a minute?
   B: Of course, Jenny. Come into my office. So, what can I do for you?
   A: Err, well, I'm working late every night at the moment...
   B: Mm, yes, I'm sorry about that. Thank you for all your hard work.
   A: The thing is... I hardly see my children now. They're in bed when I get home.
   B: Right, I see. So you'd like to finish work earlier?
   A: Oh, well, yes. If that's possible...
   B: Well, I'm sure we can do something about it.
4 A: Hey Marlena, what are you doing?
   B: What do you think? I'm studying.
   A: Oh. Why? We don't have any classes this week.
   B: Yeah, I know. But I have a lot of work to do for this project.
   A: Well, you can still eat! Come outside – we're all having lunch. You can work later!
   B: Sorry Sean, I can't. I really need to do this.
   A: Well, fine. See you later, then.

T2, p. 41, Exs 1 & 2

1 A = assistant   F = Frank
   A: Hello, Cycle Centre. How can I help you?
   F: Oh, hello, my name's Frank Parker. I'm phoning about my cycling jacket. Is it ready?
   A: Err, what colour is it please?
   F: It's grey with some black on it.
   A: Just wait a minute, please... Hello? Yes, we have a grey jacket here. It's grey and white.
   F: Oh... my jacket definitely has some black on it.
   A: Yes, there are some black lines.
   F: That sounds like it! Can I come and get it this afternoon? Are you open?
   A: Yes, until quarter past six.
   F: Great, thanks a lot. Bye.
2 F = Frank   T = Teresa
   F: Right then, what's next?
   T: Hello?
   F: Hi Teresa, it's Frank.
   T: Oh, hi Frank, how are you?
   F: Fine thanks. Listen, is Marco there? It's about cycling tomorrow.
   T: Oh, no, he isn't here at the moment, he's at the supermarket. But he says he can give you a lift at half past seven tomorrow morning.
   F: Oh, good. Thanks, Teresa.
   T: Marco's really excited. Oh yeah, and David wants to come too.

F: Great, it'll be more fun with a group of us!
T: Hope you have a good time.
F: Thanks. See you soon.
T: Bye!
3 G = George   F = Frank
   G: Hello, this is George Parker. I can't answer the phone right now, but please leave a message after the beep...
   F: Hi Dad? It's me... Are you there? Listen, there's a really nice flat for you in Tindall Street. It has one bedroom, so it's quite small, but it's comfortable. The best thing? There's a garage so you can park your car there. I can't visit it with you tomorrow because of the cycling trip. But are you free on Monday morning? Maybe we can go and see it then? Anyway, bye for now.

7.1, p. 43, Ex 5

1 In Mexico City, a taxi is a green Volkswagen Beetle!
2 In London, the subway is called the Underground and in Paris it's called the Métro.
3 Carl Benz is famous for making the first car in 1885.
4 The first plane trip, in 1904, was only five minutes long.
5 In Shanghai, you can take a very fast train called a 'maglev' from the city centre to the airport.

7.2, p. 46, Ex 2

1 A: Oh no! We just missed the train. When's the next one?
   B: There's another one in about an hour.
2 A: Hi, this ticket machine is out of order. Is there another one?
   B: No, you need to go to the ticket office over there.
3 A: Can I have a receipt, please?
   B: Yes, of course. Here you are.
4 A: Excuse me, how long does it take to get to the city centre?
   B: About 10 minutes.
5 A: Hi, can you take me to the station, please?
   B: Sure, but which one – bus or train?

7.3, p. 46, Exs 3 & 4

1 A: Hey Rob, how are you? How was Iceland?
   B: Hmm, not so good, really.
   A: Oh no, why? When we went to Iceland, we had a great time. We went to see the Northern Lights, visited Reykjavik... It was beautiful.
   B: Yes, it was beautiful. But it was very dark! In the mornings, it was dark until 10 a.m. Then there were a few hours of daylight, but it was dark again by four in the afternoon!

84

A: Oh no, I guess February isn't the best time to go there. We didn't have that problem in May.
  B: Well, I didn't really mind the dark days, actually. The problem was the evenings. We didn't do very much because all the restaurants and bars were closed. Most evenings we stayed in the hotel and watched TV!
  A: Mm, that's a shame.
2 A: So, where do you want to go on holiday?
  B: How about Kerala? It looks beautiful in these pictures...
  A: Kerala? Where's that?
  B: Oh come on! It's in India, in the south. There are lovely beaches and the food's incredible.
  A: Hmm, sounds perfect. I'm sure it's too expensive for us though.
  B: No, the prices for August are really cheap. It's a good deal!
  A: Mm, yeah. OK then! What's the weather like there?
  B: It says... Ah. August is in the monsoon season – 'it rains all day for months'. The best weather is between November and February – not too hot and not too wet.
  A: Mm, we can't go away then. Let's choose a different place.
3 A: So, how was your holiday, Marta?
  B: Great, thanks! We had a really good time. California's an incredible place!
  A: What did you do there?
  B: A lot! We went to the beach, we went walking in the national parks, we had a few days in San Francisco... It was all so beautiful. I loved all the places we visited.
  A: Wow! And I'm sure the weather was fantastic – really hot and sunny?
  B: Yeah, it was definitely hot! Some days it was too hot for me – I just stayed inside. That was the only way to stay cool! If I go again, I don't think I'll go in July. Maybe October instead – it's still warm at that time of year, but it doesn't get so hot!

 8.1, *p. 48, Ex 3*

1 editor
2 presenter
3 photographer
4 reporter
5 journalist
6 cameraman / camerawoman

8.2, *p. 51, Ex 8*

On Monday, I arrived at the newspaper offices very early. First I met Michael, one of the journalists. Then Michael introduced me to the other people in the office. Later, I met Marcia, the editor of the newspaper. I was really nervous! On Monday, my only job was making coffee! On Tuesday, Marcia finally gave me some more interesting things to do. I enjoyed my week at the newspaper but, in the end, I decided that journalism isn't the job for me.

8.3, *p. 52, Ex 2*

1 A: I crashed the car.
  B: Oh no! That's awful!
2 A: We're engaged!
  B: Are you? Congratulations!
3 A: I won some money!
  B: Really? How much?
4 A: I passed my exams!
  B: That's great news! Do you want to go to university next?
5 A: I feel really ill.
  B: Oh no! I'm sorry to hear that.

 8.4, *p. 52, Ex 1*

1 You need to wear warm clothes if you go outside today – the weather is quite cold, with icy conditions in some areas of the country.
2 A: So, Mandy, how did you feel when you won the competition?
  B: Well, I didn't know people liked my book so much, so I was really surprised!
3 I'm here in the Swiss Alps to learn more about an incredible building project. In the past, travelling through these mountains was slow and difficult. But now all that is changing...
4 Now let's go to Galgenwaard where Liverpool are playing Utrecht... Hi, Liam, what's the score so far?

 8.5, *p. 52, Exs 2 & 3*

1 You need to wear warm clothes if you go outside today – the weather is quite cold, with icy conditions in some areas of the country. Temperatures are a lot lower than yesterday: it's just four degrees in Berlin and it'll be a rainy day for people in the capital. In Frankfurt it's cold too, but the day looks dry and bright. In Munich...
2 A: So, Mandy, how did you feel when you won the competition?
  B: Well, I didn't know people liked my book so much, so I was really surprised! And very happy, of course. This is my first writing prize, so it's very exciting.
  A: Mm, yes... And do you know what you want to do with your prize money?
  B: Well, before the competition, I didn't have a lot of money. So it's a long time since I last went on holiday – the first thing I want to do is go away and relax!
  A: You definitely deserve it! Well, Mandy, thank you...
3 I'm here in the Swiss Alps to learn more about an incredible building project. In the past, travelling through these mountains was slow and difficult. But now all that is changing... Two thousand metres under the ground, engineers are building a tunnel through the mountains – it's 57 kilometres long! When the tunnel opens in 2018, trains will travel between Milan and Zurich in only two and a half hours. That's faster than travelling by plane! We spoke to one of the engineers...
4 A: Now let's go to Galgenwaard where Liverpool are playing Utrecht... Hi, Liam, what's the score so far?
  B: Thanks, Kate. It's an exciting match here today, with two goals scored in the first ten minutes! Both teams are playing well, but Utrecht has the support of the crowd – there are a lot of Dutch fans here today... And that's the whistle. As we go into half time, the score stands at one all...

9.1, *p. 55, Ex 4*

1 savoury   5 disgusting
2 spicy   6 creamy
3 healthy   7 filling
4 sweet   8 delicious

9.2, *p. 58, Ex 2*

C1 = customer 1   W = waiter
C2 = customer 2

C1: Hi, can we have a table for two, please?
W: Sure, here you are. Can I get you something to drink?
C2: Yes, can we have two glasses of red wine, please? And a bottle of water.
W: Certainly.

W: Are you ready to order?
C1: Yes. To start with, I'd like the tomato salad, please.
W: Tomato salad, OK. And for you?
C2: Can I have the antipasti, please?
W: That's fine. And for your main courses?
C1: Er, I'd like the lasagne, please.
C2: And can I have the steak, please? With chips.
W: OK, coming right up.

W: Can I take your plates?
C1: Yes, of course. Thank you.
W: Would you like to see the dessert menu?
C2: No, thank you. Can we have the bill, please?
W: One moment, please... Here you are.
C2: Thank you. Can I pay by card?
W: Yes, of course. That's no problem.

85

TRANSCRIPTS

9.3, p. 58, Ex 1

Hello and welcome to Meals in Minutes! For this week's simple recipe you need one small onion, some tomatoes, salt and pepper, some good quality spaghetti and, finally, Parmesan cheese. With these simple ingredients, we're going to make a delicious Italian dish, pasta napolitana...

9.4, p. 58, Exs 2 & 3

Hello and welcome to Meals in Minutes! For this week's simple recipe you need one small onion, some tomatoes, salt and pepper, some good quality spaghetti and, finally, Parmesan cheese. With these simple ingredients, we're going to make a delicious Italian dish, pasta napolitana...

So, first of all, cut up the onions and tomatoes. Put them in a pan and add some fresh black pepper. You need to cook these for about 10 minutes, until the vegetables are soft. Next, cook the pasta in about two litres of boiling water. It's a good idea to add some salt to the water, too. When the pasta is ready (after about eight minutes), throw away the cooking water. Then, mix the pasta with the tomatoes and onions. Finally, put the pasta on a plate and add the cheese. You can add some more pepper as well, if you like. And that's it, a delicious dinner in 15 minutes!

T3, p. 61, Exs 1 & 2

1   Oh, erm... I had toast and a cup of coffee. Two big slices of toast... with some olive oil and a few slices of tomato. And I had some juice, too... orange juice.

2   Er, breakfast in Egypt is very healthy. There's always yoghurt and cream cheese. And bread, too... We have that with the cheese and maybe some cucumber or olives. Oh, and egg.

3   Well, err, I have four children and we always have breakfast together before school and work. So it's always very noisy! But I love it, it's our way of saying 'Good morning' and being together as a family.

4   I had breakfast really early today because I took my son to the airport. He's going on holiday. So... I suppose it was about five thirty. Yes, that's right... because we left the house at six.

5   What? Every day? Um, no, I'm not usually hungry in the morning. I always have a cup of tea, though... And I do eat breakfast at the weekends, when I have more time.

10.1, p. 63, Ex 7

1   upload, download
2   turn off, turn on
3   plug in, unplug
4   switch on, switch off

10.2, p. 66, Ex 1

1   send a text message
2   click on the menu
3   key in a name
4   press the red button
5   select 'video'

10.3, p. 66, Exs 1–4

1   **A:** Oh ... why isn't this working?
    B: What happens if you click that... hmm. Well, the light's on.
    A: I know, but I can't see them... I can hear their voices though.
    B: Hang on ... Look! What's that down there? There they are – you made the screen too small!
    A: Oh, sorry! Hi, Zainab, we can see you now!

2   **A:** So, you type in the address and then it gives you the directions for where you want to go.
    B: Hey, that's good, really useful. I'd love one like that! I'm always lost.
    A: Anyway, let's go. The film starts in 10 minutes so we need to get there quickly.
    B: Mm, OK. So... you turn right at the traffic lights...
    A: Yeah, then take the next left.

3   **A:** Hello?
    B: Hi, it's me. We just finished, so I wanted to call you quickly.
    A: How was it, then?
    B: Uh, don't ask me about it! I don't want to talk about it!
    A: Oh no, was it that bad? After all that studying that you did!
    B: I know, but I studied all the wrong things! There were a lot of questions I didn't know the answer to – and there was a question from that ONE class I didn't go to!
    A: That was bad luck – it sounds awful! Did you answer any of the questions?
    B: I answered some of them, but not enough. It was a disaster!
    A: I'm sure you did better than you think!

11.1, p. 71, Ex 5

Angie: This is my third year in this job, and I feel like I need a change. I might start looking for a new job soon, but I'm worried that it'll take a long time because the economy isn't very strong at the moment.

Tomoko: Next year will definitely be an important year for me. I'm going to finish my university degree and I need to decide what to do next. It might not be easy to get a job – a lot of my friends had problems finding work.

Samir: I'm going to start a new job next week – I'm excited but a bit nervous, too. I won't know any of the other people, so I keep asking myself: 'Will I get on with them?' I hope they're nice!

Geoff: The company had a good year this year, so we might get a bonus – if we're lucky! But if we do, I won't spend it on something expensive like a holiday – I think it's more important to save it for the future.

11.2, p. 72, Ex 1

1   Can you answer the phone for me?
2   Let me buy you a coffee.
3   I'll get that for you.
4   Can you help me with the cooking?
5   Will you close the window, please?
6   I'll call you this evening!

11.3, p. 72, Exs 1–4

T = Tim   A = Anna

T: Hey Anna, what's up? Are you OK?
A: Yeah, I'm OK. It's just this job – it's so boring!
T: Oh, come on. It's only cleaning. And you don't need to do it for long... You'll be happy when you have more money for university.
A: I know, I know. But it's hard work! At least it's only part-time, I suppose. It's just, I keep thinking about your first job... That was a lot more interesting!
T: Mm, working in Paris was incredible, but the job, well, it wasn't easy.
A: Really? I thought you liked working at the museum?
T: I did, yeah... I mean, it was satisfying talking to the visitors, helping them... But I was always tired – I worked from 8 a.m. to 7 p.m., so it was a really long day.
A: Hmm. The salary was good though, right?
T: Uh, not really. And living in Paris was expensive! At least you're still living at home with mum and dad. That way you can save more money.
A: I guess. My job's not exactly well-paid though!
T: No... but, you know, the money will still help. And you only need to work for one more month!
A: Yeah, you're right... Not much longer!

86

12.1, p. 74, Exs 4 & 5

1 **A:** OK, sir. So that's one double room, for the nights of the 17th and 18th of March.
   B: That's great. Thank you. Oh, one more thing... How far is the hotel from the train station?
   A: Oh, it's not far – about a twenty-minute walk. But the best thing to do is to take a taxi from the station.

2 **A:** Good afternoon, Sanderson-Brown Limited. How can I help you?
   B: Good afternoon. I'd like to speak to Lisa Sanderson, please.
   A: I'm afraid Mrs Sanderson is out of the office at the moment. She's having lunch with some clients. Can I take a message?

3 **A:** What did you decide to do about the job, Ollie? Are you going to accept it?
   B: I still don't know. I don't know if it's what I want to do.
   A: I understand. I didn't know whether to leave my last job. So, I sat down and made a list of all the good and bad things about it. That really helped – I left the next day!

4 **A:** What do you want to eat tonight? Any suggestions?
   B: Um, how about a takeaway? Chinese, maybe?
   A: To be honest, I feel like doing some cooking. Something really nice, for a change.

5 **A:** My dad's really excited. He's going to retire next week.
   B: That's great, Laura! What's he going to do? Start a new hobby?
   A: I'm not sure. He and mum want to have a holiday. Then they'll see what happens when they get home.

12.2, p. 77, Ex 7

1 When I was younger I always went to bed late, but now I like an early night!
2 I hated living in a small place when I was a teenager.
3 I can live in the country and still work at a school in the city.

12.3, p. 78, Ex 2

1 **A:** So Gianni, can you recommend a good place to eat? I'll book a table for tonight.
   B: Good idea! There's a great Turkish restaurant about five minutes away. It's really popular.
   A: That sounds great! Have you ever eaten there?
   B: No, I haven't, but everyone says the food is amazing. I'd like to try it!

2 **A:** Excuse me, can you help us? We're looking for somewhere to have a drink near here.
   B: Well, you're in the right place! This area's famous for its nightlife.
   A: Really? That's good. Where do you recommend?
   B: Well, my favourite bar is The Lounge. It's just around the corner.
   A: Sounds good! What's it like?
   B: Relaxed atmosphere, great music... You'll love it!

12.4, p. 78, Exs 1–3

In this week's programme about amazing achievements, we look at the life of Mark Beaumont, a man who is famous for cycling around the world.

When he was a child, Mark lived in Scotland. At the age of 12, he cycled across this country. Then, a few years later, he completed a 1,400-kilometre journey through the whole of the United Kingdom. Mark's next journey, from the top to the toe of Italy, was even longer!

After university, Mark planned his biggest adventure yet. He decided to cycle around the world! Mark completed his amazing journey on the 15th of February, 2008, when he cycled under the Arc de Triomphe in Paris. In total, the journey took 194 days and 17 hours. During the trip, Mark travelled through some very difficult conditions. Two things that helped him were the blog he wrote each day and the video diary he made.

Two years after this, Mark started another incredible journey: he cycled over 20,000 kilometres across the Americas, from Alaska to southern Argentina. It wasn't an easy ride! Mark had problems with illness and bad weather. The most amazing thing? He didn't just cycle; he also stopped on the way to climb the two highest mountains in the Americas!

At the moment, Mark is travelling around the UK, talking to people about his journeys. He says he's planning another trip soon, he just won't tell us where it is!

T4, p. 81, Exs 1 & 2

P = presenter   **J** = Jim   **M** = Maggie
P: Let's welcome Jim and Maggie Truman! Now, Maggie, have you been married for a long time?
M: Oh, yes, about ten years.
P: Wow, you must know each other very well. And Jim, what do you both do?
J: Well, at the moment I'm unemployed... Maggie makes the money in our house. She's an accountant for a big company in Chicago.
P: Right! So, Jim, I'm going to ask you four questions about Maggie. Then Maggie will answer the questions, too. If your answers are the same, you score a point. Is that clear?
J/M: Oh, yes. / Very clear, thanks.
P: OK, Maggie, can you go behind the screen? Thank you. Now Jim, what's Maggie's favourite gadget?
J: Oh, that's easy. I gave her an iPod for her birthday. She goes jogging with it all the time.
P: OK, next question: How many different countries has your wife visited?
J: Um, let me think. Only two, I think, she doesn't really like travelling. Yes, two – Canada and Mexico.
P: OK. And third question: what's her favourite place in the world?
J: Oh, it's definitely Chicago – she loves her home town.
P: OK, and last question: What are your plans for the summer?
J: Well, we're going to Ireland to stay with my cousins.
P: OK, that's great! Thank you, Jim! Now, Maggie, are you ready?
M: Yes!
P: OK, the first question I asked Jim was: What's your favourite gadget?
M: My favourite gadget? Well... my new digital camera probably. No! That's wrong! Jim bought me an iPod for my running – I love it!
P: That is... correct! The next question was: how many different countries have you visited?
M: Well, I don't travel a lot now, but I loved travelling when I was younger... Let me see, Mexico, Brazil, France, Egypt, Thailand... So about eight, probably.
P: Hmm, that's not what Jim said! He said... two! But don't worry, you can still win if you get the next two questions right. What's your favourite place in the world?
M: Well ... it has to be Paris – it's the most beautiful city I've ever visited!
P: Are you sure Maggie? Because Jim said you love your hometown Chicago the most!
M: Oh, err...
P: What a shame! That means that Peter and Aurelia are this week's winners! Before you go, Maggie, what are your plans for the summer?
M: We're going to New York. I'm going to run the marathon. And Jim's going to watch...
J: Er... I thought we were going to Ireland...
P: So... I'm afraid that's all we've got time for this week...

TRACK LISTING

TRANSCRIPT	CONTENT	TRACK
7.1	Page 43, Exercise 5	21
7.2	Page 46, Functional language, Exercise 2	22
7.3	Page 46, Listening, Exercises 3 & 4	23
8.1	Page 48, Exercise 3	24
8.2	Page 51, Exercise 8	25
8.3	Page 52, Functional language, Exercise 2	26
8.4	Page 52, Listening, Exercise 1	27
8.5	Page 52, Listening, Exercises 2 & 3	28
9.1	Page 55, Exercise 4	29
9.2	Page 58, Functional language, Exercise 2	30
9.3	Page 58, Listening, Exercise 1	31
9.4	Page 58, Listening, Exercises 2 & 3	32
T3	Page 61, Progress test 3, Listening	33
10.1	Page 63, Exercise 7	34
10.2	Page 66, Functional language, Exercise 1	35
10.3	Page 66, Listening, Exercises 1–4	36
11.1	Page 71, Exercise 5	37
11.2	Page 72, Functional language, Exercise 1	38
11.3	Page 72, Listening, Exercises 1–4	39
12.1	Page 74, Exercises 4 & 5	40
12.2	Page 77, Exercise 7	41
12.3	Page 78, Functional language, Exercise 2	42
12.4	Page 78, Listening, Exercises 1–3	43
T4	Page 81, Progress test 4, Listening	44